John Cann Bailey

Studies in Some Famous Letters

John Cann Bailey

Studies in Some Famous Letters

ISBN/EAN: 9783337817398

Printed in Europe, USA, Canada, Australia, Japan

Cover: Foto ©Thomas Meinert / pixelio.de

More available books at **www.hansebooks.com**

STUDIES

IN

SOME FAMOUS LETTERS

BY

J. C. BAILEY

LONDON
THOMAS BURLEIGH
1899

BRADBURY, AGNEW, & CO. LD., PRINTERS,
LONDON AND TONBRIDGE.

PREFACE.

OF the following Essays, two—those on Lady Mary Wortley Montagu and on Edward FitzGerald—first appeared in "The Quarterly Review"; one—that on Gray—in "Murray's Magazine"; the study of Cowper in "Macmillan's Magazine"; and that of Gibbon in the "Fortnightly Review." A few slight alterations and corrections have been made in reprinting them. With these exceptions, they are republished in their original form; and, for permission to do this, I am indebted, in the several cases, to the courtesy of Mr. Murray, Messrs. Macmillan & Co., and Messrs. Chapman & Hall, which I take this opportunity of acknowledging.

The Essays on Swift, Johnson, and Lamb appear now for the first time.

I will only add that, in venturing to publish a volume of this sort, I have had one principal consideration in my mind. It is that, as it seems to me, Letters, whether regarded simply as a form of Literature, or as affording not the least sure material for the study of character, have not, at the present time, as many readers as they may fairly claim to deserve. I hope I have not neglected their purely literary importance, but my more immediate object has certainly been to piece together, as far as may be, the scattered fragments of self-portraiture, which are to be found in every collection of Letters. The picture, with which they provide us, cannot, perhaps, be of the quite finished and full-length order: but it should at least not fail to give us the authentic outlines, faithfully sketched, of the characters and characteristics of some men and women in whom the world will always take a natural and legitimate interest.

J. C. BAILEY.

CONTENTS.

STUDIES

IN

SOME FAMOUS LETTERS.

COWPER.[1]

IT is often said that the delightful art of letter-writing is dead. No doubt circumstances are not so favourable to it as they once were, as they were, for instance, in the last century, the golden age of the letter-writer. It never does to have too much of a good thing, and so Rowland Hill, and Penny Posts, and hourly deliveries, have very nearly killed the old-fashioned letter which rambled and gossiped and wandered at will up and down all sorts of subjects, overflowing

[1] First printed in " Macmillan's Magazine," Nov., 1891. Cowper's Letters are to be found, for the most part, in Southey's " Life and Works of William Cowper," in fifteen volumes, 1835. There is also an excellent selection by Canon Benham, published in Messrs. Macmillan's " Golden Treasury Series," 1884.

into every corner of the paper except just
the little space required for the address on
one side and the seal on the other.   When
you paid fourpence, or sixpence, or more, for
a letter, or had had the trouble of asking
a Parliamentary acquaintance for a frank,
you naturally took your money's worth.
And then in the last century everybody
seems to have had plenty of time ; nowadays we are all in a hurry from morning
to night.   And hurry, which ruins nearly
everything from bootlaces to epic poems,
is no friend to letters, though not so fatal
to them as to more ambitious productions.
Byron may dash down on his paper, in his
headlong, helter-skelter sort of way, the
last witticisms and personalities that
happen to be simmering in his excited
brain, and the effect is very characteristic
and very telling.   But the best letters
cannot be written so.   Hurry and exuberance of this kind weary in the end, and
leave an uncomfortable sensation of disorder and unrest in the mind ; the highest
productions of every kind, in art, or music,
or literature, however intense may be the
immediate delight they give, leave the
mind to settle in the end into a sort of
quiet enjoyment.   The pleasure over, we
rest in calm satisfaction.   And this must

be the law in letter-writing, as in everything else, if letters are to be read. They can only rank as literature by submitting to conditions to which literature submits. And there will not only be the general conditions attached to all composition to be taken into account, but special conditions attached to this particular form of composition. It is at first sight a little doubtful what the characteristics of a good letter are. Some people think it merely a matter of conversation through the post; and there is certainly a good deal to be said for this theory, for the elaborately composed letter is the worst possible letter. Ease and naturalness, lightness of touch, the sense for the little things which are the staple of conversation and correspondence as well as of life, the ever-present consciousness that one is simply one's self and not an author or an editor, are of all qualities the most essential in a letter. A good letter is like a good present—a link between two personalities, having something of each in it. It is emphatically from one man, or woman, to another, in contrast, for instance, to a newspaper, which is from nobody or anybody to anybody or nobody. But if this were all, Byron would be incontestably the best of our letter-writers. Nothing could possibly be more personal, and characteristic and spontaneous, than his letters: his likes and dislikes, his pleasures and disappointments, his passing fancies, schemes, whims, are poured out in them with a force and freshness which are unrivalled and inimitable. It is just as if he were talking, and talking with the freedom and openness of a man at a friendly supper-party; and of course his evident frankness doubles the interest and importance of it all. But after all writing is not talking, and an exuberance which might perhaps be delightful, when broken by other voices and lighted up by all the play of eye and feature, becomes after a time intolerable in a volume of letters. It is the same thing, I suppose, as one sees in portraits, where a too energetic or spirited attitude nearly always produces failure. Whatever makes a claim to permanence must have at least a suggestion of repose about it.

English literature is fairly rich in good letters, and in the very first rank of the best come the letters of the recluse, who might naturally be supposed to have nothing to write about, the quiet, retiring, half-Methodist poet, William Cowper. They are written in the most beautifully easy English, and he steers his way with unfailing instinct between the opposite dangers of pompousness and vulgarity, which are the Scylla and Charybdis of the letter-writer.. They are not set compositions, but he never forgets that he is writing, not talking; they contain long discussions, yet he does not often forget that he is writing a letter and not a book. The most striking proof of his wonderful gifts in this direction is the story of his life. He was not a leading figure in the world of fashion, like Horace Walpole and Lady Mary Wortley Montagu; he was not even a scholar or a man of letters with intellectual friends, like Gray and Fitz-Gerald; still less had he been behind the great political curtain like Chesterfield, or travelled everywhere and been the talk of all the world like Byron. Nearly all his letters are written upon the most ordinary subjects to the most ordinary people, and written either from Olney, which was certainly a very dull place, or from Weston Underwood, which cannot have been a very lively one. And yet I doubt if a volume so good and readable as Mr. Benham's "Selected Letters of Cowper" in the "Golden Treasury Series" could be made out of those of any

one else. Not even Gray, I fancy, in spite
of the fascination of his character and
the delicate charm of his humour, in spite
of the combination of real learning with
those high gifts of imagination and sensibility which make him a unique figure in
the last century, has left so many letters
likely to retain a permanent interest as
Cowper. Gray's letters are delightful, as
is everything of his, but simply as letters
they do not seem to me quite so perfect as
Cowper's. Nor is the reason perhaps very
hard to find. Other things being equal,
of two writers or painters the one who has
chosen the better subject will clearly succeed best. Now Cowper of all writers of
letters has the best subject, because he
has no subject at all. And so he is led
into quiet gossiping self-revelation, little
humorous touches about himself and his
correspondents, the nothings that filled up
their lives as they fill up ours, their likes
and dislikes, their sayings and doings,
their comings and goings. Human nature
is always and everywhere of the same stuff,
and the glimpses these letters give us of
kind old Mrs. Unwin, and "my dearest
Coz" Lady Hesketh, and "Mrs. Frog,"
and "Johnny" Johnson, and, fullest and
best of all, of "your humble me, W. C.,"

can never lose their interest, because the human nature they show us is the same as we see around us every day, and as our sons and grandsons will see too when we have vanished in our turn as completely as Cowper and his friends. Not that, of course, mere accuracy is enough in drawing human nature,—that may be found—is found often enough—in the dullest and most insipid novels; it is when the eye to see is found in company with the power of feeling life's joys and sorrows, and with the gift for telling the ta[le] the books are written which nev[er go] out of date. Few men have ha[d these] gifts more fully than Cowper, and [it is a] pity that he never wrote a novel. If he had done so, we might have the two sides of English middle-class life in the country and the country towns drawn in one picture; the simple goodness of the immortal Vicar side by side with the delightful vanity and self-importance of Mrs. Bennett and Mrs. Allen. Perhaps, too, the creator of Sir Roger de Coverley might have found a successor; for Cowper recalls Addison on more than one point, in the quiet reserve which gives such charm to his humour, and in the delicacy of his touch as well as in the ease and purity of his English. Meanwhile the letters are the only substitute we have for the unwritten novel, and there could not be a better.   It would not be easy to find a more charming exhibition of the novelist's gift of making us at once at home in the world to which he wishes to introduce us, than this little letter of Cowper's to his cousin, Lady Hesketh, before her first visit to him at Olney. We have only to read its few sentences, and we can hardly fail to carry away with us a fairly clear idea of what manner of man he was, a fairly true picture of him and his life and ways and surroundings, and, what is much more, a disposition to like him and sympathise with him, and a wish to know more of him. The novelist who can accomplish his introductory duties as well is a happy man; and certainly I cannot find anything which will serve better as an introduction both to Cowper and to his letters.   Here it is:

"And now, my dear, let me tell you once more that your kindness in promising us a visit has charmed us both. I shall see you again. I shall hear your voice. We shall take walks together. I will show you my prospects, the hovel, the alcove, the Ouse and its banks, everything that I have described. Talk not of an inn! Mention it not for your life! We have never had so many visitors but we could easily accommodate them all ; though we have received Unwin, and his wife, and his sister, and his son, all at once. My dear, I will not let you come till the end of May, or beginning of June, because before that time my greenhouse will not be ready to receive us, and it is the only pleasant room belonging to us. When the plants go out we go in. I line it with mats, and spread the floor with mats ; and there you shall sit with a bed of mignonette at your side, and a hedge of honeysuckles, roses, and jasmine ; and I will make you a bouquet of myrtle every day. Sooner than the time I mention the country will not be in complete beauty. And I will tell you what you shall find at your first entrance. Imprimis, as soon as you have entered the vestibule, if you cast a look on either side of you, you shall see on the right hand a box of my making. It is the box in which have been lodged all my hares, and in which lodges Puss[1] at present. But he, poor fellow, is worn out with age, and promises to die before you can see him. On the right hand stands a cupboard, the work of the same author ; it was once a dove-cage, but I transformed it. Opposite to you stands a table, which I also made. But a merciless servant having scrubbed it till it became paralytic, it serves no purpose now but of ornament ; and all my clean shoes stand under it. On the left hand, at the farther end of this superb vestibule, you will find the door of the parlour, into which I will conduct you, and where I will introduce you to Mrs. Unwin, unless we should meet her before, and where we will be as happy as the day is long. Order yourself, my cousin, to the ' Swan ' at Newport and there you shall find me ready to conduct you to Olney.

[1] Cowper's tame hare.

My dear, I have told Homer what you say about casks and urns, and have asked him whether he is sure that it is a cask in which Jupiter keeps his wine. He swears that it is a cask, and that it will never be anything better than a cask to eternity. So if the god is content with it, we must even wonder at his taste, and be so too.—Adieu! my dearest, dearest cousin,—W. C."

Did ever poet's cousin have prettier welcome? There is nothing clever in the letter, nothing much to catch the eye or explain the fascination, and yet every time we read it we like it the better. Where does the charm lie? Perhaps in the choice and delicate English Cowper always employs; perhaps in the simple prettiness of the picture, or, it may be, in the perfect, if unconscious, firmness and delicacy with which it is executed; more likely still, perhaps, in the attraction exercised upon us by Cowper's own overflowing good-nature, which seems to have an affectionate word not only for his cousin and his hares, but for everything about him down to the mignonette and the roses and the honeysuckle, and even the poor paralytic table.

This letter belongs to the happiest period of his life, the time one naturally goes to when one wishes to see him most himself. If we are to date him by a *floruit* after the fashion of the Greek and Latin poets, 1786, the year in which this letter was written, would be almost exactly his central year. But his letters are not confined to that happy time, and we can, if we like, almost follow him all through his life with their help. I have given a frontispiece, as it were, from his years of health and fame and quiet happiness; but we had better now go back to the beginning, and take things orderly as they come.

His life is broken into very simple divisions. He was born at Berkhampstead Rectory in 1731, went to school at Westminster, and entered at the Middle Temple in 1748. London was his home till 1763, when he first went out of his mind. He seems to have lived a pleasant enough life while in London, not much troubled with the law, but spending his time in a careless sort of fashion with young literary men like himself, among whom were Lloyd and Colman, and perhaps Churchill. Probably he was much like other young men who lived in the Temple in those days, when it was said of it: "The Temple is stocked with its peculiar beaux, wits, poets, critics, and every character in the gay world; and it is a thousand pities that so pretty a society should be disgraced with a few dull fellows who can submit to puzzle themselves with cases and reports." From 1763 to 1765 he was in an asylum ; and it was there that, on recovering, he first received those strong religious impressions which coloured the rest of his life. He lived at Huntingdon from 1765 to 1767, most of the time with the Unwins, a clergyman's family with whom he became very intimate. After Mr. Unwin's death in 1767, he and Mrs. Unwin moved to Olney, where they stayed till 1786. Here his poetry was mainly written, though his happiest days were probably those spent at Weston Underwood, a country village not far from Olney, to which Lady Hesketh persuaded them to move in 1786. There he stayed till 1795, and only left it because his terrible malady was so plainly returning that his young cousin, John Johnson, wished to have him with him in Norfolk where he could be always by his side. There he remained in different houses, but always in the same melancholy state, till the end came at Dereham in April, 1800.

There are very few letters of the London period extant, but one of the few is so characteristic of Cowper and his easy, good-natured, sensible way of looking at life, that I must quote some of it. It is, if possible, truer and timelier in our day than it was in his ; for there seems to be no more universally accepted doctrine nowadays than that the whole of life is to be absorbed in getting, or, equally often in unnecessarily increasing, the material means of life ; no time being lost on life itself, in the higher meaning of the word. Cowper and Thurlow were in early years in the same attorney's office. Perhaps after all to us who look back on it now, the obscure and comparatively poor poet may seem to have got as much out of life as the Lord Chancellor ! There may even be people bold enough to maintain that Cowper's life was better worth living than Thurlow's even if his poetry had been a failure.

But here is the letter or part of it :

" If my resolution to be a great man was half so strong as it is to despise the shame of being a little one, I should not despair of a house in Lincoln's Inn Fields, with all its appurtenances : for there is nothing more certain, and I could prove it by a thousand instances, than that every man may be rich if he will. What is the industry of half the industrious men in the world but avarice ? and, call it by which name you will, it almost always succeeds. But this provokes me, that a covetous dog, who will work by candle-light in the morning to get what he does not want, shall be praised for his thriftiness, while a gentleman shall be abused for submitting to his wants, rather than work like an ass to relieve them. . . . Upon the whole, my dear Rowley, there is a degree of poverty that has no disgrace belonging to it ; that degree of it, I mean, in which a man enjoys clean linen and good company ; and, if I never sink below this degree of it, I care not if I never rise above it. This is a strange epistle, nor can I imagine how the devil I came to write it : but here it is, such as it is, and much good may you do with it."

There are naturally no letters while he was at St. Alban's, but they begin again as soon as he gets to Huntingdon. His experiences of keeping house for two persons are like other people's before and since :

"DEAR JOE, [he is writing to Joseph Hill, who was his business adviser through life, and the best of friends as well].—Whatever you may think of the matter, it is no easy thing to keep house for two people. A man cannot always live upon sheep's heads and liver and lights, like the lions in the Tower ; and a joint of meat in so small a family is an endless incumbrance. My butcher's bill for the last week amounted to four shillings and tenpence. I set off with a leg of lamb, and was forced to give part of it away to my washerwoman. Then I made an experience upon a sheep's heart, and that was too little. Next I put three pounds of beef into a pie, and this had like to have been too much, for it lasted three days, though my land-lord was admitted to a share of it. Then as to small beer, I am puzzled to pieces about it. I have bought as much for a shilling as will serve us at least a month, and it is grown sour already. In short, I never knew how to pity poor housekeepers before: but now I cease to wonder at the politic cast which their occupation usually gives to their countenance, for it is really a matter full of perplexity."

Huntingdon must have seemed a quiet place after London, but Cowper seems to have settled down easily enough.

"Here is a card assembly," he writes, "and a dancing assembly, and a horse race, and a club, and a bowling green, so that I am well off, you perceive, in point of diversions; especially as I shall go to 'em just as much as I should if I lived a thousand miles off."

The chief attraction to him was apparently the river.

"The river Ouse,—I forget how they spell it— is the most agreeable circumstance in this part of the world: at this town it is, I believe, as wide as the Thames at Windsor: nor does the silver Thames better deserve that epithet, nor has it more flowers upon its banks, these being attributes, which, in strict truth, belong to neither. Fluellen would say, they are as like as my fingers to my fingers, and there is salmon in both. It is a noble stream to bathe in, and I shall make that use of it three times a week, having introduced myself to it for the first time this morning."

Having given bits from these letters to Hill, I ought not to omit what may be regarded as, in a certain sense, the other side of the picture. In the earnestness and enthusiasm of his new-born religious feelings, he had entered with the Unwins on a course of life which was very dangerous to one who had suffered as he had, and which indeed was not long in showing itself so. This is how they lived:

"We breakfast commonly between eight and nine: till eleven we read either the Scripture, or the sermons of some faithful preacher of those holy mysteries: at eleven we attend divine service, which is performed here twice every day: and from twelve to three we separate and amuse ourselves as we please. During that interval I either read in my own apartment, or walk, or ride, or work in the garden. We seldom sit an hour after dinner: but, if the weather permits, adjourn to the garden, where, with Mrs. Unwin and her son, I have generally the pleasure of religious conversation till tea-time. If it rains, or is too windy for walking, we either converse within doors, or sing some hymns of Martin's collection: and, by the help of Mrs. Unwin's harpsichord, make up a tolerable concert, in which our hearts, I hope, are the best and most musical performers. After tea, we sally forth to walk in good earnest. Mrs. Unwin is a good walker, and we have generally travelled about four miles before we see home again. At night we read and converse as before till supper, and commonly finish the evening either with hymns or a sermon, and last of all the family are called to prayers."

Well might Lady Hesketh say afterwards, with reference to days spent in similar fashion with Mr. Newton: "to such a tender mind, and to such a wounded yet lively imagination, as our cousin's, I am persuaded that eternal praying and preaching was too much." There are, no doubt, some specially gifted spiritual natures who can literally obey the "Think of God more frequently than you breathe" of Epictetus, or the "Pray without ceasing" of St. Paul; but they are the rare exceptions who combine the saint's love of God and sense of sin with an ease and cheerfulness of temperament which in any one else would be called Epicurean. The attempt to enforce such a life produces, if the first of these qualities be wanting, the cold and formal religion of the monk of the fifteenth century; if the second be absent, as in Cowper's case, it produces melancholy or despair.

Less than a year after this letter was written Mr. Unwin died, and Cowper and Mrs. Unwin went to live at Olney. They stayed there nearly twenty years, and through Cowper's letters we are as well acquainted with their life there as if we had been their next door neighbours. His way of noting and describing all sorts of details and small matters, which other people would have passed over, makes our picture of the little house at Olney and its inhabitants as complete as an interior by Teniers or Ostade; only fortunately the inhabitants are rather more attractive than the boors who are too often the only figures in Dutch pictures. A neat and careful gentleman of the eighteenth century like Cowper, particular about his wigs and buckles being of the fashionable shape, was not likely to crowd his canvas with the drunken ostlers and ploughmen of Olney. His subjects are himself and his friends, and after them just the first thing besides, whatever it might be, that came into his head. Here is his theory of letter-writing:

"My dear Friend,—You like to hear from me: this is a very good reason why I should write. But I have nothing to say: this seems equally a good reason why I should not. Yet if you had alighted from your horse at our door this morning, and at this present writing, being five o'clock in the afternoon, had found occasion to say to me, 'Mr. Cowper, you have not spoke since I came in: have you resolved never to speak again?' it would be but a poor reply if in answer to the summons I should plead inability as my best and only excuse. And this by the way suggests to me a seasonable piece of instruction, and reminds me of what I am very apt to forget, when I have any epistolary business in hand, that a letter may be written upon anything or nothing, just as that anything or nothing happens to occur. A man that has a journey before him twenty miles in length, which he is to perform on foot, will not hesitate and doubt whether he shall set out or not, because he does not readily conceive how he shall ever reach the end of it : for he knows that by the simple operation of moving one foot forward first, and then the other, he shall be sure to accomplish it. So it is in the present case, and so it is in every similar case. A letter is written as a conversation is maintained, or a journey performed : not by preconcerted or premeditated means, a new contrivance or an invention never heard of before, —but merely by maintaining a progress, and resolving as a postilion does, having once set out, never to stop till we reach the appointed end. If a man may talk without thinking, why may he not write upon the same terms ? A grave gentleman of the last century, a tie-wig, square-toe, Steinkirk figure would say—' My good Sir, a man has no right to do either.' But it is to be hoped that the present century has nothing to do with the mouldy opinions of the last : and so, good Sir Launcelot, or Sir Paul or whatever be your name, step into your picture frame again, and leave us moderns to think when we can and to write whether we can or not, else we might as well be dead as you are."

The difficulty in writing about letters is that to illustrate one must quote ; and then, as the charm of letters lies, or ought to lie, in the large, the quotation of a line or two, which is often enough in poetry, does not do justice to the letter-writer, and we have to quote nearly in full—which again demands a magnificent disregard of considerations of space.   However, this letter which I have just been giving, seemed to me to have nearly irresistible claims, for not only is it the best account of Cowper's ideas about writing letters, but it is less accessible than many others. Mr. Benham, who has got most of the best letters in his selection, has left this one out.

Cowper's letters are generally characterised by a sort of careless, easy inevitableness, but he could go out of his way to *make* a letter sometimes.   Here is a bit of rhyming *tour de force* sent to Mr. Newton. Its subject is his first volume of poems, and it is curious to note how, for all its cleverness, it remains a perfect letter with the true Janus-face looking back to the writer and on to the recipient ; the rhyme is just the sort of joke Cowper liked ; the careful explanation that the poems were written " in hopes to do good " is as plainly the Newtonian part of the affair.   It begins, " My very dear friend, I am going to send, what when you have read, you may scratch your head, and say, I suppose, there's nobody knows, whether what I have got, be verse or not,—by the tune and the time, it ought to be rhyme ; but if it be, did you ever see, of late or of yore, such a ditty before?" This sort of thing is kept up all through the letter and then he ends up: "I have heard before, of a room with a floor, laid upon springs, and such like things, with so much art, in every part, that when you went in, you was forced to begin a minuet pace, with an air and a grace, swimming about, now in and now out, with a deal of state, in a figure of eight, without pipe or string, or any such thing; and now I have writ, in a rhyming fit, what will make you dance, and as you advance, will keep you still, though against your will, dancing away, alert and gay, till you come to an end of what I have penned; which that you may do, ere Madam and you are quite worn out with jigging about, I take my leave, and here you receive a bow profound, down to the ground, from your humble me, W. C."

A letter like this is worth giving, because it is probably unique in the annals of the art; but it is the less striking letters that are really more characteristic of Cowper. The best are those which we hardly notice the first time we read them, but like better every time we take them up. One of the most charming of the letters from Olney is the second he wrote to Lady Hesketh when John Gilpin had induced her to begin their old correspondence again. This is how he ends it :

" I have not answered many things in your letter, nor can do it at present for want of room. I cannot believe but that I should know you, notwithstanding all that time may have done. There is not a feature of your face, could I meet it upon the road by itself, that I should not instantly recollect. I should say, that is my cousin's nose, or those are her lips and her chin, and no woman upon earth can claim them but herself. As for me, I am a very smart youth of my years. I am not indeed grown gray so much as I am grown bald. No matter. There was more hair in the world than ever had the honour to belong to me. Accordingly, having found just enough to curl a little at my ears, and to intermix with a little of my own that still hangs behind, I appear, if you see me in an afternoon, to have a very decent head-dress, not easily distinguished from my natural growth : which being worn with a small bag, and a black ribbon about my neck, continues to me the charms of my youth, even on the verge of age. Away with the fear of writing too often. Yours, my dearest cousin, W. C.

" P.S. That the view I give you of myself may be complete, I add the two following items, that I am in debt to nobody, and that I grow fat."

But perhaps the most inimitable and delightful of all Cowper's epistolary virtues is his power of telling stories. Everybody has felt how little power the ordinary story-teller, whether on paper or in conversation, has of making us go with him, and see the thing as he sees it. Cowper's stories are as alive for us as they were for his friends. Take for instance this little account of a country election in the old days :

"We were sitting yesterday after dinner, the two ladies and myself, very composedly, and without the least apprehension of any such intrusion, in our snug parlour, one lady knitting, the other netting, and the gentleman winding worsted, when, to our unspeakable surprise, a mob appeared before the window, a smart rap was heard at the door, the boys hallooed, and the maid announced Mr. Grenville. Puss was unfortunately let out of her box, so that the candidate, with all his good friends at his heels, was refused admittance at the grand entry, and referred to the back door, as the only possible way of approach. Candidates are creatures not very susceptible of affronts, and would rather, I suppose, climb in at a window than be absolutely excluded. In a minute, the yard, the kitchen, and the parlour were filled. Mr. Grenville, advancing towards me, shook me by the hand with a degree of cordiality that was extremely seducing. As soon as he, and as many more as could find chairs were seated, he began to open the intent of his visit. I told him I had no vote, for which he readily gave me credit. I assured him I had no influence, which he was not equally inclined to believe, and the less, no doubt, because Mr. Ashburner, the drapier, addressing himself to me at that moment, informed me that I had a great deal. Supposing that I could not be possessed of such a treasure without knowing it, I ventured to confirm my first assertion by saying that if I had any I was utterly at a loss to imagine where it could be, or wherein it consisted. Thus ended the conference. Mr. Grenville squeezed me by the hand again, kissed the ladies, and withdrew. He kissed likewise the maid in the kitchen, and seemed upon the whole a most loving, kissing, kind-hearted gentleman."

There are very few pictures of life in the last century where the figures stand out of the canvas so clear, direct, and natural, with their own personality about them, as they do here. And how charmingly Cowper's humour lights up the whole picture! He is always amusing about himself and his own importance, and gives us a number of little touches on the subject which are worth noting. He had no poetic contempt for personal adornment; when his friend Unwin is going up to town, he writes to him: "My head will be obliged to you for a hat, of which I enclose a string that gives you the circumference. The depth of the crown must be four inches and one eighth. Let it not be a round slouch, which I abhor, but a smart, well-cocked, fashionable affair." ·

His fame too, when it came, amused him very much, and he is never tired of joking about it. "I cannot help adding a circumstance that will divert you. Martin [an innkeeper] having learned from Sam whose servant he was, told him that he had never seen Mr. Cowper, but he had heard him frequently spoken of by the companies that had called at his house, and therefore when Sam would have paid for his breakfast, would take nothing from him. Who says that fame is only empty breath? On the contrary it is good ale and cold beef into the bargain." So again, and neither of these are given by Mr. Benham, who, no doubt, could not find room for all the good things,—" I have been tickled with some *douceurs* of a very flattering nature by the post. A lady unknown addresses the best of men ; —an unknown gentleman has read my inimitable poems, and invites me to his seat in Hampshire ;—another incognito gives me hopes of a memorial in his garden, and a Welsh attorney sends me his verses to revise, and obligingly asks,

> " ' Say, shall my little bark attendant sail,
>   Pursue the triumph, and partake the gale ? '

" If you find me a little vain hereafter, my friend, you must excuse it, in consideration of these powerful incentives, especially the latter: for surely the poet who can charm an attorney, especially a Welsh one, must be at least an Orpheus, if not something greater." And he tells Lady Hesketh : " I have received an anonymous complimentary Pindaric Ode from a little poet who calls himself a schoolboy. I send you the first stanza by way of specimen.

" ' To William Cowper, of the Inner Temple, Esq., of his poems in the second volume.
" ' In what high strains, my Muse, wilt thou
Attempt great Cowper's worth to show ?
Pindaric strains shall tune the lyre,
And 'twould require
A Pindar's fire
To sing great Cowper's worth,
The lofty bard, delightful sage,
Ever the wonder of the age,
And blessing to the earth.'

" Adieu, my precious cousin, your lofty bard and delightful sage expects you with all possible affection."

But we are getting now, indeed have already got, so far as some of the letters I have been quoting are concerned, into the Weston Underwood period of the poet's life, where he is at his happiest and best, enjoying his success and fame, and the many friendships, both old, re-opened and new-discovered, which his fame brought him, busy at his Homer with a fixed quantity to translate every day, so that he always writes in " Homer hurry,"—a kind of hurry which somehow

produces the most lazy, delightful letters
—occupied and amused, in fact, in such
a fashion that his melancholy found no
loophole to get in by till Homer was
finished and despatched, Mrs. Unwin
aging every day and often suffering, and
only the uncongenial task of editing
Milton was there to save him from himself. We will not follow him there,
except in sympathy; indeed, after a very
few more specimens of his " divine chit-
chat," as Coleridge called it, I must
take my leave of him altogether, and
bring this paper to an end. I have given
one specimen of his story-telling powers.
Here is another, this time to Mrs. Throckmorton, the wife of the Squire of Weston
Underwood :

" My dear Mrs. Frog,—You have by this time
(I presume) heard from the Doctor, whom I desired
to present to you our best affections, and to tell you
that we are well. He sent an urchin (I do not mean
a hedgehog, commonly called an urchin in old times,
but a boy, commonly so called at present), expecting
that he would find you at Bucklands, whither he
supposed you gone on Thursday. He sent him
charged with divers articles, and among others with
letters, or, at least, with a letter : which I mention
that, if the boy should be lost together with his
despatches, past all possibility of recovery, you may
yet know that the Doctor stands acquitted of not
writing. That he is utterly lost (that is to say, the

boy, for the Doctor being the last antecedent, as
the grammarians say, you might otherwise suppose
that he was intended) is the more probable, because
he was never four miles from his home before,
having only travelled at the side of a plough-team:
and when the Doctor gave him his direction to
Bucklands, he asked, very naturally, if that place
was in England.   So what has become of him
Heaven knows!   I do not know that any adventures have presented themselves since your
departure worth mentioning, except that the rabbit
that infested your Wilderness has been shot for
devouring your carnations; and that I myself have
been in some danger of being devoured in like
manner by a great dog, namely, Pearson's.   But I
wrote him a letter on Friday informing him that
unless he tied up his great mastiff in the daytime,
I would send him a worse thing, commonly called
and known by the name of an attorney.   When I
go forth to ramble in the fields I do not sally, like
Don Quixote, with a purpose of encountering
monsters, if any such can be found: but am a
peaceable poor gentleman, and a poet, who mean
nobody any harm, the fox hunters and the two
Universities of this land excepted.   I cannot learn
from any creature whether the Turnpike Bill is
alive or dead: so ignorant am I, and by such
ignoramuses surrounded.   But if I know little else,
this at least I know, that I love you and Mr. Frog:
that I long for your return, and that I am, with
Mrs. Unwin's best affections, Ever yours, W. C."

I am afraid I am showing the magnificent disregard of considerations of
space of which I spoke just now, but the
temptation to give this letter in full was

too great; it has always seemed to me so perfectly easy and charming, and it gives a delightful glimpse into the happiness of those early days at Weston and the pleasant intimacy that existed between the Lodge and the Hall. The Lodge wrote complimentary verses to the Hall, and the Hall (in the person of Mrs. Throckmorton and her Roman Catholic chaplain, the *Padre* of whom Cowper got very fond) transcribed the Lodge's translation of Homer; Cowper and Mrs. Unwin dined constantly with the "Frogs" and the "Frogs" occasionally with them, and altogether life seems to have passed very agreeably. Poor Cowper got into trouble for it with Mr. Newton, who did not like Roman Catholics, and kept a careful watch over his flock; but the poet could stand on his dignity when he pleased, and he would not give up his new friends; and as the *Padre* did not apparently even attempt a conversion, no harm came of it.

The two most important of the friend-ships Cowper made in the latter part of his life were those with Hayley, who was afterwards his biographer, and with his young cousin John Johnson, who took charge of him during his melancholy

closing years, and proved himself in every
way unwearying in his devotion. He
was a Cambridge undergraduate when
his cousin first made his acquaintance,
and his high spirits and good-nature
made Cowper take to him at once. The
poet liked to get him to Weston for his
vacations, and he seems to have brightened
everybody up when he stayed there. The
letters to him are nearly always bright
and cheerful. Here is one of the last
of the really happy ones. It is headed
" Io Pæan ! "

" My dearest Johnny,—Even as you foretold,
so it came to pass. On Tuesday I received your
letter, and on Tuesday came the pheasants: for
which I am indebted in many thanks, as well as
Mrs. Unwin, both to your kindness, and to your
kind friend Mr. Copeman.

> " In Copeman's ear this truth let Echo tell,—
> Immortal bards like mortal pheasants well.
> And when his clerkship's out, I wish him herds
> Of golden clients for his golden birds.

" Our friends the Courtenays have never dined
with us since their marriage, *because* we have never
asked them : and we have never asked them *because*
poor Mrs. Unwin is not so equal to the task of
providing for and entertaining company as before
this last illness. But this is no objection to the
arrival here of a bustard : rather it is a cause for
which we shall be particularly glad to see the
monster. It will be a handsome present to them.

So let the bustard come, as the Lord Mayor of London said to the hare, when he was hunting,— ' Let her come, a' God's name, I am not afraid of her.' Adieu my dear cousin and caterer—My eyes are terribly bad, else I had much more to say to you."

Not very long after this letter was written, Mrs. Unwin's health of body and mind entirely broke down, and her affection, which had so long been the greatest of blessings to Cowper, became all at once the very reverse, for she insisted on his spending his days in her room, reading to her and writing for her —occupations which had always tried him ; and as she could hardly speak, and he was thrown in this way entirely on her society, he naturally relapsed into the old melancholy. Lady Hesketh found him in 1794 in a terrible state of insanity, refusing food, walking incessantly up and down his room, filled with the most awful imaginations. Then they took him to Norfolk in the next year, and unhappily he lived on till April 25th, 1800. The despair lasted up to the moment of death; but it is consoling, as well as curious, to know, that from that moment " the expression with which his countenance settled was that of calmness and com- posure, mingled, as it were, with holy surprise." And certainly, as Southey says, "never was there a burial at which the mourners might, with more sincerity of feeling, give their hearty thanks to Almighty God, that it had pleased Him to deliver the departed out of the miseries of this sinful world."

Cowper's letters are so perfectly easy and simple and sincere that we can enjoy them in whatever mood we may happen to be, just as we can alway enjoy "Guy Mannering" or "Emma." And we enjoy them simply for their own sake. Half the interest of Lord Chesterfield's letters lies in what he regarded as his philosophy of life; Horace Walpole is at least as important from the point of view of the student of social and political history as from that of the lover of letters, and Gray too has a great deal to tell us which would be interesting and important in a book. The great merit of Cowper in this line is that he is not a philosopher, or a politician, or a scholar, but simply and solely a writer of letters. He has no extraneous claims on our interest, and indeed he became one of the best, if not the very best, of English letter-writers by simply not trying to become anything else. Never were letters written with

less idea of publication. He destroyed
all he received, and asked his correspondents to do the same with his. The letters
would never have been published but for
the success of the poems; but it is possible
that there are many people now who are
tempted to renew their forgotten acquaintance with Cowper as a poet by learning
from his letters how delightful he was
as a man.

GRAY.[1]

Gray has some claim to be considered the most universally interesting of the better known figures in our literary history. For one thing, though by far the least productive of our greater poets, he is the author of the most popular poem in the language. But that is not the only respect in which his position is unique. Lovers of poetry in this country may be roughly divided into two camps: those whose favourite study is the great line of imaginative poets which stretches from Chaucer to Milton, and again from Wordsworth to the present day, and those whose bent lies rather among the prose poets from Dryden to Johnson. No one, of course, could pretend that Gray arouses in us anything like the "wonder and astonishment" which are the tribute paid always and everywhere, without question

[1] First printed in "Murray's Magazine," April, 1891. Gray's Letters occupy the second and third volumes of Mr. Edmund Gosse's "Works of Thomas Gray," Macmillan, 1884.

or hesitation, to the transcendent powers
of Shakespeare ; or the reverent gratitude,
not unmingled with some touch of awe,
which we feel in presence of Milton's lofty
character, or when listening to the solemn
and stately march of his great poem. But
of Shakespeare himself we know little or
nothing, and none dare presume to be
familiar with Milton. He is a prophet
and master to all, and no man's intimate.
But, 'if we put these greater men aside,
Gray may seem, of all the poets whom we
know well, the most generally interesting,
for he has the singular advantage of
belonging, in some sort, to both the
groups into which our poets naturally fall,
and possessing attractions which appeal
to both parties. We know Johnson better,
no doubt, and Pope and Cowper as well,
but Pope cannot get away from the eighteenth century, the fascination of Johnson
seems incapable of crossing the Channel,
and Cowper was altogether a lesser man
than Gray. Gray, too, of course, belongs
to his century as every man must, and has
its characteristic features. No one can
read his letters without seeing that the
silly sort of gossip in which the men and
women of his day so specially delighted,
had its attractions for him. And the spirit

of the age has everywhere, or almost everywhere, left its mark upon his poetry.
What can be more completely in that
spirit, for instance, that spirit, too, at its
very worst, than such a passage as—

> " The star of Brunswick smiles serene,
>   And gilds the horrors of the deep."

Then we find him thinking Le Sueur
almost equal to Raphael, a piece of pure
eighteenth century criticism, and failing
altogether to appreciate Collins. There
could be no more striking proof, considering how much he and Collins had in common with each other, and in contrast with
every other poet of the time, of the extent
to which he shared the prejudices of his
age. The remarkable thing, however, the
thing which gives him his unique interest,
is that he was not altogether of his time;
that though living with Mason and Walpole, he could step into a sphere never
entered, or so much as dreamt of, by them
or the. men they most admired. There
is no need to go farther than that very
Installation Ode in which the " Star of
Brunswick . . . gilds the horrors of the
deep," to find proof that Gray had in him
something not only better than bombast
of this sort, but belonging to an altogether

different, an infinitely purer and truer, order
of ideas.   Who would believe that—

> " Sweet is the breath of vernal shower,
>   The bees' collected treasures sweet ;
>   Sweet music's melting fall, but sweeter yet
>   The still small voice of gratitude "—

was written before even the birth of Wordsworth ?   Or, again, what could more completely mark the poet inspired by Nature,
as opposed to the poet whose mainspring
is his own cleverness, or the praise of " the
town," than such lines as—

> " There pipes the woodlark, and the song-thrush there
>   Scatters his loose notes in the waste of air."

It is only fair to insist on this side of
Gray's character and poetical position,
because an attempt has been made to
deny it in the most recent book about him.
Mr. Tovey, in his little volume called
" Gray and his Friends," has given us, in
the first place, a fairly complete picture of
West, and Gray's friendship for him, made
up from their correspondence, and from
various compositions of West's which have
survived ; secondly, some new letters of
Gray, none of which, however, are of
great interest ; and lastly, some " Notes
on Travel," which Mr. Gosse had justly
called " rather dry and impersonal," and

a few miscellaneous fragments in prose and verse. No doubt where so little is left of an interesting figure, as in Gray's case, it is very tempting to publish all that we can get hold of; but the modern rage for printing and giving to the world with an air of great importance every trivial scrap of paper that bears the name of a poet, or of any of his relations or friends, even though it be nothing but a laundress's bill, or a note of orders to a servant, has not much to recommend it, and I am not sure that there is a great deal of real interest in what Mr. Tovey has published. Much that is curious there is, certainly, and nothing that lovers of Gray can regret; but there is, at the same time, nothing that can claim a permanent place as literature. The Gray and West correspondence is interesting; but Gray's letters were already well known, and West's letters and frag- ments are only remarkable as showing that he was a most amiable and even charming man, in every respect a worthy friend for Gray. They cannot give him any inde- pendent place in literary history. Nothing is gained by crowding the gallery of litera- ture with pretty portraits of people who, however agreeable and amiable, have no real place there. Still, no doubt there is

no harm in publications of this sort, and
the book has its interest, if not for the
lover of literature, at least for the lover of
Gray. But it is to be regretted that
Mr. Tovey, in adding to our knowledge
of Gray and his circle, should have thought
it necessary to try to undo the effect of
the best appreciation Gray ever received.
Every one remembers Matthew Arnold's
essay on Gray, in which he took for his
text the remark made after Gray's death
by Brown—"He never spoke out." "Gray,
a born poet, fell upon an age of prose."
" Born in the same year with Milton, Gray
would have been another man ; born in the
same year with Burns, he would have been
another man."   " On the contrary," says
Mr. Tovey, " he would have been the same
man, but a less finished artist, if he had been
born in 1608."   " On whatever times he
might have fallen, if he had attempted to
sing of contemporary kings and battles,
Apollo would have twitched his ear."   Mr.
Tovey, in fact, insists that Gray's sterility
was in himself, not in his surroundings.

Now it is only reasonable to require considerable evidence before setting aside the
deliberate judgment of a man like Matthew
Arnold in such a matter as this. Long
training, working on a critical faculty so

 Gray.

rich and penetrating as his, gives to a man's judgments almost the inevitableness and certainty of instinct; and this would be especially the case in dealing with a poet like Gray, with whom Matthew Arnold had a curious affinity. Then it is fair also to say that it is not a question of kings and battles, contemporary or otherwise. Gray would have found his subject, if he could have found heart to sing with in that chilling atmosphere. It was not a song, but a voice, that he wanted. "A sort of spiritual east wind was at that time blowing: neither Butler nor Gray could flower. They never spoke out." I do not think that any one who reads Gray's poems with anything like care or thought can miss the fact that the cast of his mind was entirely different from that of the men of his day, and that he was conscious of this himself. But if the poetry is not conclusive in itself —and it must be conceded that his poetical language is, in the main, that of his time —the letters, and the picture they give of his life, leave no doubt at all about the matter. It is perfectly clear that his thoughts and ways and doings were not as those of other eighteenth century men. He anticipated the imaginative revival which was to follow at the end of the

century in more points than one. He
studied and loved the old English poetry
long before Percy's "Reliques" made such
studies the fashion ; he delighted in mountain scenery, and went through great
discomforts to enjoy it, in an age when to
all other men the Alps were simply a gloom
and a horror : he was one of the earliest
lovers of Gothic architecture, and, in his
most famous work at least, he appeared as
a poet of Nature among the crowd of wits
and poets of the town. To him the Wye
is full of " nameless wonders "; a mountain is a " creature of God," and the
Grande Chartreuse a scene " that would
awe an atheist into belief." The beautiful
and perfect Alcaic Ode, " O tu severi religio
loci," which he wrote in the monks' album
at the Chartreuse, is well known, though
not so well known as it should be. Rarely,
if ever, has so much genuine and deep
feeling been expressed in a language not
the author's own. Can it really be supposed that a man of this sort did not lose
by being placed in the first half of the last
century ? Is it not as certain as anything
can be in the study of human minds, that
Gray would have greatly gained by living
under the inspiration of Milton, or in the
companionship of Wordsworth and Cole-

ridge ?   That single striking phrase, "a creature of God," applied as Gray applied it, is proof enough, and more than enough. There is in it the germ of all that Wordsworth felt and taught.   It is too late now to put the clock back.   Matthew Arnold's brilliant essay let in in a moment a flood of light upon Gray, and showed him as he was, silent and alone, with no friend, it must always be remembered, who was able really to understand him.   No protest can be too strong against any attempt to close the shutters again and restore the old darkness.   The serious attempt to understand the minds and the exact positions of our poets must always be a difficult one ; and it is too much to ask us to go back upon an onward step once taken.

I have said that the letters of Gray throw great light on the peculiar position he held in his time ; and so they do. But they have besides a rare interest and charm of their own, and it is of that that I wish to speak more particularly now. Gray's letters are, in fact, among the very best in the language. Lovers of literature will not, perhaps, find their choice of language so delightfully and quite unconsciously perfect as Cowper's : and Gray had not Cowper's gift of retaining throughout life a child's intense pleasure in little things, which is one of the chief reasons that make the picture given in Cowper's letters so complete and finished, and the charm of them at once so simple and so lasting. Men who see even so much of the great world as Gray saw generally lose, consciously or unconsciously, the beautiful traits which childhood will, here and there, under other circumstances, hand on to mature age. Nor did the spring of Gray's humour bubble up so pure and clear and constant as Cowper's. But then Cowper's lighter letters are the best letters in the language. Gray need not fear comparison with any one else. No one can deal with large questions in a larger spirit than he can, when he chooses : he has, too, a genuine power of description : he is full of the love of Nature, especially of birds and flowers, which he studies with the methodical watchfulness of a man of science, as well as with the love of a poet : notes on art and literature, often of rare insight and power, are scattered everywhere in his letters: and then, if none of all these things interest us, there is the interest of his perpetual picture of himself and his friends, and what they thought and said and did.

I cannot begin better than with one or two of these sketches he gives of himself. He is quite at his best in them, his unbosomings, like those of many reserved men, if very rare, being also very full and frank. Of course only the most intimate friends were favoured with them, and probably even to them he would never have made up his mind to *say* half so much as he could, now and then, put on paper from a safe distance. Every shy man has felt the pleasure of writing what he knows he would die rather than say. And so I suspect even West and Wharton knew him best from his letters, or, at least, so far as he ever helped them to the key of his curious character, it was most likely to be in the occasional confessions to be found in his letters to them. To them, more than to any of his other friends, I think. West is plainly the friend he was nearest to in his earliest years: and the letters to Wharton, whom he once addresses as " My dear, dear Wharton, which is a dear more than I give anybody else," have the most easy and intimate sound of any in later life. Here is a bit of one of the earliest extant letters, telling West what he thought of Cambridge:

"You must know that I do not take degrees, and, after this term, shall have nothing more of college impertinencies to undergo, which I trust will be some pleasure to you, as it is a great one to me. I have endured lectures daily and hourly since I came last, supported by the hopes of being shortly at full liberty to give myself up to my friends and classical companions, who, poor souls! though I see them fallen into great contempt with most people here, yet I cannot help sticking to them, and out of a spirit of obstinacy (I think), love them the better for it; and, indeed, what can I do else? Must I plunge into metaphysics? Alas, I cannot see in the dark; nature has not furnished me with the optics of a cat. Must I pore upon mathematics? Alas! I cannot see in too much light—I am no eagle. It is very possible that two and two make four, but I would not give four farthings to demonstrate this ever so clearly; and if these be the profits of life, give me the amusements of it."

We get a fairly good idea of one side of Gray from this; but we may add to it a more complete portrait which was sent to West from Florence four years later.

"As I am recommending myself to your love, methinks I ought to send you my picture; you must add, then, to your former idea, two years of age, a reasonable quantity of dulness, a great deal of silence, and something that rather resembles, than is, thinking; a confused notion of many strange and fine things that have swum before my eyes for some time, a want of love for general society, indeed, an inability to it. On the good side, you may add a sensibility for what others feel, and indulgence for their faults and weaknesses, a love of truth, and detestation of everything else. Then you are to deduct a little impertinence, a little laughter, a great deal of pride, and some spirit. These are all the alterations I know of, you perhaps may find more."

A less carefully analysed and more poetical picture is one he sent to Horace Walpole, while on one of his earliest visits to the Stoke and Burnham country, which was to become so inseparably associated with his name. He says he has arrived safe at his uncle's,

" Who is a great hunter in imagination ; his dogs take up every chair in the house, so I am forced to stand at this present writing ; and though the gout forbids him galloping after them in the field, yet he continues still to regale his ears and nose with their comfortable noise and stink. He holds me mighty cheap, I perceive, for walking when I should ride, and reading when I should hunt. My comfort amidst all this is, that I have at the distance of half-a-mile, through a green lane, a forest (the vulgar call it a common) all my own, at least as good as so, for I spy no human thing in it but myself. It is a little chaos of mountains and precipices ; mountains, it is true, that do not ascend much above the clouds, nor are the declivities quite so amazing as Dover cliff; but just such hills as people who love their necks as well as I do may venture to climb, and crags that give the eye as much pleasure as if they were more dangerous. . . . At the foot of one of these squats ME, I (il penseroso), and there grow to the trunk for a whole morning. The timorous hare and sportive squirrel gambol around me like Adam in Paradise before he had an Eve; but I think he did not use to read Virgil, as I commonly do there."

There may be something of art in the drawing of a picture like this; but an artist naturally uses all his powers when he paints himself: and no one can deny the charm of the effect produced. And its being sent to Horace Walpole is a proof, if proof were needed, of the genuineness of their friendship in those early days before the quarrel. Gray evidently feels that he is writing to one who will both understand and appreciate his delight in what he describes.

But if we are to let Gray talk of anything but himself we must pass on. Every one has read and admired his excellent literary judgments. In speaking of Aristotle or Socrates, or again in speaking of Froissart, he was of course exactly in his own province: no man ever had a clearer idea of the qualities which do, and those which do not, entitle a book to claim a place as literature. But his freshness and directness, and the unconscious determination to see things as they really are which always marks a powerful mind, give a real interest and value to what he says on subjects not so

strictly within his own province.   Take
what he says of the arguments of
Materialism.

" That we are indeed mechanical and dependent
beings, I need no other proof than my own feelings;
and from the same feelings I learn, with equal
conviction, that we are not *merely* such, that there
is a power within that struggles against the force
and bias of that mechanism, commands its motion,
and, by frequent practice, reduces it to that ready
obedience which we call *Habit;* and all this in
conformity to a preconceived opinion (no matter
whether right or wrong) to that least material of all
agents, a Thought."

Could we have a better picture, more
coldly and cruelly direct, of that impene-
trable rock of common-sense against
which the most persistent, the most
apparently triumphant, determinism beats
itself in vain ?

The same good sense, which he deals
out in judgment on books and philosophies,
he can apply also to practical matters
like the choice of a profession.   Here is
a bit from a long letter of affectionate
advice sent from Florence to West, who
did not find the legal atmosphere of the
Temple particularly congenial.

" Examples shew one that it is not absolutely
necessary to be a blockhead to succeed in this
profession.   The labour is long, and the elements
dry and unentertaining; nor was ever anybody

(especially those that afterwards made a figure in it) amused or even not disgusted in the beginning; yet upon a further acquaintance, there is surely matter for curiosity and reflection. It is strange if, among all that huge mass of words, there be not somewhat intermixed for thought. Laws have been the result of long deliberation, and that not of dull men, but the contrary; and have so close a connection with history, nay, with philosophy itself, that they must partake a little of what they are related to so nearly. Besides, tell me, have you ever made the attempt? . . . Are you sure, if Coke had been printed by Elzevir and bound in twenty neat pocket volumes, instead of one folio, you should never have taken him for an hour, as you would a Tully, or drank your tea over him? I know how great an obstacle ill spirits are to resolution. Do you really think, if you rid ten miles every morning, in a week's time you should not entertain much stronger hope of the Chancellorship and think it a much more probable thing than you do at present? . . . To me there hardly appears to be any medium between a public life and a private one; he who prefers the first, must put himself in a way of being serviceable to the rest of mankind, if he has a mind to be of any consequence among them. Nay, he must not refuse being in a certain degree even dependent upon some men who are so already. If he has the good fortune to light on such as will make no ill use of his humility, there is no shame in this: if not, his ambition ought to give place to a reasonable pride, and he should apply to the cultivation of his own mind those abilities which he has not been permitted to use for others' service. Such a private happiness (supposing a small competence of fortune) is almost always in every one's power."

S.   E

Gray himself nominally entered upon the study of the law ; but only nominally ; his choice was very soon made in favour of "private happiness " and the " cultivation of his own mind." And if in this early letter his bias seems to be somewhat in favour of the law and a public career, twenty years later it had become as distinctly the other way. We find him saying to Wharton :—

" To find oneself business (I am persuaded) is the great art of life ; and I am never so angry, as when I hear my acquaintance wishing they had been bred to some poking profession, or employed in some office of drudgery, as if it were pleasanter to be at the command of other people, than at one's own ; and as if they could not go, unless they were wound up. Yet I know and feel, what they mean by this complaint : it proves that some spirit, something of genius (more than common) is required to teach a man how to employ himself."

Whatever other genius Gray had, there is no doubt he was remarkably possessed of this genius of self-employment. He likes talking of his laziness, as every student does, but his labours must have been immense. Nowadays that we are all specialists, and a man who knows anything of physics is indignant at the supposition of his having had any time to learn his Greek alphabet, we can only hold

our breath in silent awe when we are told
that Gray had not only thoroughly read
and digested the books that made up the
literature of the world, but was also a
really learned archæologist, an enthusiastic student of the history of architecture,
a pioneer to some extent by his chrono-
logical tables in the systematic study of
Greek history, a cultivated and even
learned amateur in music, and, what is
most astonishing of all to us, an acute,
patient, and genuinely scientific observer
of natural phenomena. His careful lists,
kept from day to day, of the direction of
the wind, of the heat his thermometer
registers, of the singings and flowerings
of birds and plants, would have delighted
the heart of the Meteorological and
Botanical Societies of the present day.
Take one day—April 20, 1760—from a
long list he sends Wharton.

"*April* 20.—Therm. at 60°. Wind S.W. Skylark,
chaffinch, thrush, wren, and robin singing. Horse-
chestnut, wildbriar, bramble, and sallow had spread
their leaves. Hawthorn and lilac had formed their
blossoms. Blackthorn, doubleflowered peach, and
pears in full bloom: double tonquils, hyacinths,
anemones, single wallflowers, and auriculas in
flower. In the fields, dog violets, daisies, dandelion,
buttercups, red-archangel, and shepherd's purse."

One wonders that more people who live

in the country do not realize what a delightful occupation it is to be the daily witness and companion of that eager, onward march to meet the summer which the birds and flowers make every spring! No one could devise a more innocent occupation ; and it is not one of the least useful.   A man may enjoy quiet observation of this kind, too, even if he have none of the genuine ardour of the gardener.   Gray thought he had this too, but he never had much opportunity of putting his enthusiasm to the proof.

"And so you have a garden of your own, and you plant and transplant, and are dirty and amused ; are not you ashamed of yourself? Why, I have no such thing, you monster, nor ever shall be either dirty or amused as long as I live! My gardens are in the window, like those of a lodger up three pair of stairs in Petticoat Lane or Camomile Street, and they go to bed regularly under the same roof that I do ; dear, how charming it must be to walk out in one's own garden, and sit on a bench in the open air with a fountain, and a leaden statue, and a rolling stone, and an arbour!"

That his interest in gardening was genuine and serious is proved by his procuring the mention, in one of Count Algarotti's books, of a recognition of our English skill in the matter of landscape gardening, being anxious, as he says, to "save to our nation the only honour it has in matters of taste, and no small one, since neither Italy nor France have ever had the least notion of it, nor yet do at all comprehend it when they see it."

The great charm of a collection of letters is, that it lets us see a man in nearly all his moods, and as he actually was at the moment of writing. As long as the letters are spread over a fairly wide period, and are addressed to a fairly wide circle of correspondents, they can hardly fail to tell us their tale, even when most unwilling. Insincerity, with letters as with a journal, must almost always fail, so long as they remain as originally written. When touched up, they of course become autobiographies, which may easily be very successful frauds. But give us what a man, however insincerely, wrote at a particular moment of his life, and we know, if not what he *was*, at least what he wished to appear, and that is, after all, no bad key to what he really was, especially when it can be applied frequently to almost every year of his life. It has been said by Mr. Goldwin Smith, perhaps in an unnecessarily off-hand way, that "Gray's letters are manifestly written for publication." I can see no sign of this, with regard to the great bulk of them, except that when he has described anything carefully and well in one letter, he is apt to use the same phrases in another, and that, I suppose, we all do, unconsciously if not consciously. But in any case, with so many letters and so different, I do not see how any one can doubt that we know the real Gray as he actually was in life. The variety of correspondence is a great safeguard in a matter of this kind. A man naturally writes of what he knows will interest his correspondent. And so we might never have been able to realise, to the full extent, Gray's affectionate study of the classics if we had lost the letters to West, the only one of his friends who was anything like his equal as a scholar. It would be an impossible stretch of affectation to write a letter like this to any one who was not well read in his Greek and Latin authors.

"You see, by what I sent you, that I converse as usual with none but the dead: they are my old friends, and almost make me long to be with them. You will not wonder, therefore, that I, who live only in times past, am able to tell you no news of the present. I have finished the Peloponnesian war much to my honour, and a tight conflict it was, I promise you. I have drank and sung with Anacreon for the last fortnight, and am now feeding sheep with Theocritus. Besides, to quit my figure

(because it is foolish) I have run over Pliny's
Epistles and Martial ἐκ παρέργου; not to mention
Petrarch, who, by the way, is sometimes very
tender and natural. I must needs tell you three
lines in Anacreon, where the expression seems to
me inimitable. He is describing hair as he would
have it painted.

'Ἕλικας δ' ἐλευθέρους μοι
Πλοκάμων ἄτακτα συνθεὶς
Ἄφες ὡς θέλωσι κεῖσθαι.'"

The picking out of these three lines is
proof of a power of poetic appreciation,
rare at any time, and most of all, perhaps,
at the time Gray wrote. It is the beauty
of such passages, with their wonderful
combination of richness and simplicity,
that is the reward of the Greek scholar
and the despair of the translator. We can
all see their charm when a Gray lends us his
eyes for the purpose ; but how many of us
would have seen it with our own, and pulled
up in our reading to learn them by heart ?
But, if West brings out Gray's love of
books, Wharton will produce for us the
lighter side of his character. Who would
not like to have received such a letter as
this, and gone down in obedience to
it to meet the poet " slipping " into the
Cambridge coffee-house?

" MY DEAR WHARTON,—This is only to entreat
you would order *mes gens* to clean out the apart-

ments, spread the carpets, air the beds, put up the tapestries, unpaper the frames, etc. ; fit to receive a great potentate, who comes down in the flying coach, drawn by green dragons on Friday, the 10th instant. As the ways are bad, and the dragons a little out of repair, it will probably be late when he lands, so he would not choose to be known, and desires there may be no bells, nor bonfires. But as persons incog. love to be seen, he will slip into the coffee-house. Is Mr. Trollope among you? Good lack, he will pull off my head for never writing to him, oh, Conscience, Conscience!"

Here is another letter that must have made a breakfast go down very comfortably. I suppose it is the only contemporary account of the opening of the British Museum; anyhow it is the best.

"LONDON, July 24, 1759.
"I am now settled in my new territories commanding Bedford Gardens, and all the fields as far as Highgate and Hampstead, with such a concourse of moving pictures as would astonish you; so *rus-in-urbe-ish*, that I believe I shall stay here, except little excursions and vagaries, for a year to come. What though I am separated from the fashionable world by broad St. Giles's and many a dirty court and alley, yet here is air and sunshine and quiet, however, to comfort you; I shall confess that I am basking with heat all the summer, and I suppose shall be blown down all the winter, besides being robbed every night; I trust, however, that the Museum, with all its manuscripts and rarities by the cart-load, will make ample amends for all inconveniences."

He then describes the company assembled in the reading-room on that opening day:—

"We were, first, a man that writes for Lord Royston; secondly, a man that writes for Dr. Burton of York; thirdly, a man that writes for the Emperor of Germany, or Dr. Pocock, for he speaks the worst English I ever heard; fourthly, Dr. Stukely, who writes for himself, the very worst person he could write for; and lastly, I, who only read to know if there be anything worth writing, and that not without some difficulty. I find that they printed one thousand copies of the Harleian Catalogue, and have only sold fourscore; that they have £900 a year income and spend £1300, and are building apartments for the under-keepers; so I expect in winter to see the collection advertised and set to auction."

In another letter he finishes up with: "The University (we hope) will buy," an anticipation which may cause some amusement in Great Russell Street, as may also his account of the early amenities shown by the keepers to each other.

"When I call it peaceful, you are to understand it only of us visitors, for the society itself, trustees and all, are up in arms like the fellows of a college. The keepers have broke off all intercourse with one another, and only lower a silent defiance as they pass by. Dr. Knight has walled up the passage to the little house, because some of the rest were obliged to pass by one of his windows in the way to it."

I think I have quoted enough to show how very readable Gray's letters are, both in themselves and in the pictures they give of the man and of his times. It is really not too much to say that he never wrote a dull letter. His mind is so fresh and alert, he is so open to impression from every side, so alive to see and note whatever of interest is going on about him, that his letters nearly always have about them a certain spring and motion which is peculiarly delightful. There may possibly be a few people who have grown weary of the languor and insipidity of the ordinary novel, and do not know where to go for light reading. Have they ever tried our English letter-writers? Letters cannot, no doubt, claim a very high place as serious literature, but they might fairly, one would think, carry on a successful rivalry with the fatiguing productions of our inexhaustible lady novelists. If any one has a fancy to amuse himself with society and politics, Horace Walpole will give him Duchesses and Countesses and Secretaries of State, and real ones too, to his heart's content. If his taste be country life and quiet humour, he will not find them anywhere in greater perfection than in the letters of Cowper or Edward

FitzGerald. If, like some men and many women, I believe, he reads novels to teach himself how to behave in polite society, Lord Chesterfield is the acknowledged authority in such matters, and has no objection to go into details. Or, if he be possessed of larger interests, or have an ear which asks· for a lightness of hand and sureness of touch, a power of writing English, in fact, not possessed, I fancy, by more than one or two of our living novelists, let him go to Gray, and the shy little poet of the " Elegy " may prove as interesting as many of the heroines of his previous acquaintance. At any rate his clear, pointed, vigorous language, as pure as it is firm and crisp, cannot fail of its charm. Everybody enjoys the spell of a genuine and original personality, which lives its own life and goes its own way ; and Gray was that, at least, if nothing else. In mind and character, as in trees and plants, the surest sign of life is growth ; and Gray never ceased to grow up to the very end. He was always breaking up the fallow ground, and filling in the vacant spaces all his life. " The mind has more room in it than most people seem to think, if you will but furnish the apartments," he says in one place : and in another, " the drift of my present studies is to know, wherever I am, what lies within reach that may be worth seeing, whether it be building, ruin, park, garden, prospect, picture, or monument; to whom it does, or has belonged, and what has been the characteristic and taste of different ages." He is all eager for travel, and sees that it always adds something worth having to a man. "Do not you think a man may be the wiser (I had almost said the better) for going a hundred or two of miles?" And his travelling was not only the fashionable progress through the Continental capitals; he may be called the discoverer of the mountains. When he came back from the Highlands, he said: "The Lowlands are worth seeing once, but the mountains are ecstatic, and ought to be visited in pilgrimage once a year. . . . A fig for your poets, painters, gardeners, and clergymen that have not been among them;" and neat and particular little man as he was, he was not afraid when he was fifty-two to make a walking tour alone in the Lakes, doing three hundred miles in seventeen days, if Mr. Gosse's interpretation of a passage in one of his letters is to be trusted. The journal which he wrote for Wharton records his delight in the scenery, as well as the adventures he went through.   Here is one which shows how indefatigable he was :

" Dined by two o'clock at the Queen's Head, and then straggled out alone to the *Parsonage*, fell down on my back across a dirty lane, with my glass open in one hand, but broke only my knuckles, staid nevertheless, and saw the sun set in all his glory."

The next day after this was one of his happiest : I must find room for a bit of what he says about it.

"*October* 3.—Wind at S.E., a heavenly day. Rose at seven, and walked out under the conduct of my landlord to *Borrodale*.   The grass was covered with a hoar frost, which soon melted and exhaled in a thin blueish smoke. . . . Our path tends to the left, and the ground gently rising, and covered with a glade of scattering trees and bushes on the very margin of the water, opens both ways the most delicious view that my eyes ever beheld.   Behind you are the magnificent heights of *Walla-Crag ;* opposite lie the thick hanging woods of Lord Egremont, and *Newland* valley, with green and smiling fields embosomed in the dark cliffs ; to the left the jaws of *Borrodale*, with that turbulent chaos of mountain behind mountain, rolled in confusion ; beneath you, and stretching far away to the right, the shining purity of the *Lake*, just ruffled by the breeze, enough to shew it is alive, reflecting rocks, woods, fields, and inverted tops of mountains, with the white buildings of *Keswick*, *Crosthwait* Church, and *Skiddaw* for a background at a distance.   Oh, Doctor ! I never wished more for you ! "

The enthusiasm which could carry a gouty man the wrong side of fifty through all this would be rare in our own day ; in Gray's it was quite unique, and points to a real originality of character in him. Intellectual acuteness was common enough in those days : qualities of soul, among which a love of mountain scenery may without extravagance be ranked, were not common—never indeed are common. To feel, of oneself and by oneself, and not at second hand, that God's voice is audible among the mountains in an altogether special way, to him who has but ears to hear it, is what does not come to every man, does not come indeed to any man, who has not a more than common soul. But that is just what Gray habitually felt. In the highlands of Scotland, at the Grande Chartreuse, in the roads that wind through the English lakes, it is everywhere the same : he feels that the presence of the mountains is the presence of God. His more than English reserve as to his inner life is apt to make us remember nothing of him but the variety and fascination of his intellectual gifts. But, by doing so, we lose a most real and characteristic side of his character. The same man, whose mental versatility was such that he was equally at home in pointing out to one correspondent the difference between a Lepisma and an Adenanthera, or giving another the names of the Inkfish in Greek, Latin, Italian, and French, with its place in the order of Mollusca; who made real contributions to the studies of English metre and Greek chronology; who at one moment occupies himself in compiling tables of the weather and the crops, and at another in annotating his large collection of manuscript Italian music, and whose comprehensive powers of appreciation found Socrates "divine," and the Comédie Française "beyond measure delightful," was all the while as simple as a child in the things of the inner life. He talks little about religion, and we know nothing of his views about details of doctrine, but his religious feeling was deep, genuine, and unshaken. "No very great wit, he believed in a God," is his own account of himself; and, when any of those things which unlock the secrets of every man's heart—a sorrow, an illness, a death—come upon him or his friends, we find him always the same, speaking the same simple language, breathing the same quiet spirit of resignation and hope. He knows the value of sorrow;

" Methinks I can readily pardon sickness, and age, and vexation, for all the depredations they make within and without, when I think they make us better friends, and better men, which I am persuaded is often the case. I am very sure, I have seen the best-tempered, generous, tender young creatures in the world, that would have been very glad to be sorry for people they liked, when under any pain, and could not, merely for the want of knowing rightly, what it was themselves."

And his warning to his young friend Bonstetten against the dangers of pleasure is that of a man deeply, even anxiously, in earnest.

" You do me the credit, and false or true it goes to my heart, of ascribing to me your love for many virtues of the highest rank. Would to heaven it were so! but they are indeed the fruits of your own noble and generous understanding, which has hitherto struggled against the stream of custom, passion, and ill company, even when you were but a child; and will you now give way to that stream when your strength is increased? Shall the jargon of French sophists, the allurements of painted women *comme il faut*, or the vulgar caresses of prostitute beauty, the property of all who can afford to purchase it, induce you to give up a mind and body by nature distinguished from all others, to folly, idleness, disease, and vain remorse?"

His tone about these matters is quite uniform. We find him, for instance, saying of Rousseau: " As to his religious discussions, which have alarmed the world, I set them all at nought, and wish they had been omitted." The same letter curiously enough contains two other things worth noting in the same connection. He says:

"Mrs. Jonathan told me you begun your evening-prayer as soon as I was gone, and that it had a great effect upon the congregation; I hope you have not grown weary of it, nor lay it aside when company comes."

And he adds incidentally: "Poor Mrs. Bonfoy (who taught me to pray) is dead." Still more clearly do his feelings come out in the actual presence of death: "He who best knows our nature," he says on one such occasion, "by such afflictions recalls us from our wandering thoughts and idle merriment, from the insolence of youth and prosperity, to serious reflection, to our duty and to himself." And his letter to Mason, written just when his wife lay dying, is one of the most beautiful ever written at such a moment. I must allow myself to give it in full.

"My dear Mason,—I break in upon you at a moment when we least of all are permitted to disturb our friends, only to say that you are daily and hourly present to my thoughts. If the worst be not yet passed, you will neglect and pardon me; but if the last struggle be over, if the poor object of your long anxieties be no longer sensible to your kindness or to her own sufferings, allow me (at

 Gray.

least in idea, for what could I do were I present more than this), to sit by you in silence, and pity from my heart, not her who is at rest, but you who lose her. May He who made us, the Master of our pleasures and of our pains, preserve and support you. Adieu!"

So touching a letter raises the man, for whose sorrow Gray's reserve could be so beautifully broken, into something more than poor Mason has been commonly thought to have been ; and for Gray, even if it stood alone in its kind, it would prove that he is to be remembered, not only for his rare and almost unique combination of intellectual gifts, but also for his high qualities of character and soul.

LADY MARY WORTLEY MONTAGU.[1]

Lady Mary Wortley Montagu has never received the attention she deserves as the most remarkable Englishwoman of the eighteenth century. She is that interesting personality, a combination of the typical and the exceptional. All the common characteristics of the women of her day are to be found in her, as well as qualities which can never be common in any day. She has as much of the extraordinary taste of the eighteenth century for silly and malicious personal gossip as the idlest and most ignorant woman in the fashionable world around her. There is not a trace in her of the theological interests of the sixteenth or seventeenth centuries, or of the social and philanthropic enthusiasms of the nineteenth. No one indeed entered more

[1] First printed in the " Quarterly Review," Oct., 1897. Lady Mary Wortley Montagu's Letters are to be found in her " Letters and Works," edited by Mr. W. Moy Thomas, in two volumes, Swan Sonnenschein, 1893.

fully than she did into the eighteenth century's meaning of that word "enthusiasm." She had just the way of looking at things which made Gibbon say of Law, the author of the "Serious Call"; "had not his vigorous mind been clouded by enthusiasm, he might be ranked with the most agreeable and ingenious writers of the times." The "cool and reasonable concern for themselves," which Bishop Butler urged upon his hearers, and that good-humour which, according to Shaftesbury, is not only "the best Security against Enthusiasm, but the best Foundation of Piety and true Religion," were enough for her, as they were for her contemporaries. For her, as for most of them, religion and religious "ordinances are so far sacred as they are absolutely necessary in all civilized governments," and not very much further. To endeavour to overthrow them is, for that reason, to be " an enemy to mankind "; but as for religion independently, and in itself, it was, in Lady Mary's eyes, a thing of that sort which " Thou shalt not kill, but needst not strive, Officiously to keep alive." There is no unrest of any kind in her, no discontent, divine or otherwise. She was incapable of being disturbed by any anxiety about the state of her soul, or of the poor, or of her country, or indeed by any " obstinate questionings " of any kind at all. Rich and happy as she was, and universally courted and honoured, with the good health and multiplicity of interests which together defeat the monster *ennui*, she encouraged no feelings which she could not justify to her reason, took the world very much as she found it, and learned to unite the carefully - acquired common sense of the Epicurean to the inherited complaisance of the Whig. In all this, except the good sense and the absence of vices, she is very like her contemporaries. But she is a great deal beside which they never thought of being. She is the friend of Addison, the friend, and, of course, also the enemy of Pope; she is the woman who had the courage to introduce the system of inoculation to her countrymen, and the practical kindliness to teach Italian peasants the art of making butter; who received the gift of a house from one foreign city, and refused the offer of a statue from another; above all, for us to-day, she is the bright, good - humoured, charming personality, interested in everything, and carrying our interest along with her own, born, as she says, with a passion for learning, teaching herself for want of better teachers, translating Epictetus in her childhood, and managing, in an old age of solitude and retreat, by farming and gardening, and especially by reading, never to "have half an hour heavy on hèr hands." And she is something else too, without which we should never have known anything about her at all: she is the writer of letters so easy, so bright, so intelligent, in the fullest and best sense, that it has been possible, if not for truth, at least for patriotic prejudice, to speak of them in the same breath with those of Madame de Sévigné.

That parallel cannot indeed be justified when the case is carried before the higher courts of appeal. Those who care for the finer things in literature will never be able to rise with the same feelings after reading Lady Mary as they experience when they put down a volume of Madame de Sévigné. Not only in delicacy and good taste, but in depth of character and all the qualities that make up what we think of as the "soul," Lady Mary is immeasurably inferior to her great predecessor. There could not be a clearer proof of it than her astonishing failure to see more in the letters to Madame de

Grignan than "sometimes the tittle-tattle of a fine lady, sometimes that of an old nurse, always tittle-tattle." But if she is not, in any real sense, Madame de Sévigné's equal, there are enough points of likeness between them to make the comparison inevitable. Each of them owes her fame to her letters, and knows no rival among her countrywomen in that art; each was born and lived all her life in the highest society of her day; literature was the favourite amusement of each, and good sense and good temper the favourite philosophy; each, above all, had a single strong attachment, and sent the bulk, and the best, of her letters to the daughter who was the passion of her life. Resemblances of this sort are of course superficial, not essential; and perhaps if Lady Mary had not herself invited the comparison one would sympathize with her in the accidents which made it so inevitable. However, when that has once been put aside there are few others which she need fear. In her own day and her own style she has no rival. Much indeed of the difference between her and Madame de Sévigné is due to her having lived a hundred years later. In her, as in the best known men and women of her day, the intelligence had gradually usurped an almost exclusive domination. There is nothing which she or Voltaire or Gibbon could not look at with perfect directness and serenity. Their business is with facts, and their object simply to understand and make the best of them. Practical benevolence may come into their scheme of life; Lady Mary, indeed, and others of her time and temper accomplished far more for the good of their neighbours than people before and after who have professed to be, and perhaps have actually been, full of the intensest sympathy for the lot of humanity in this world or the next. But what the typical man or woman of the eighteenth century does for others is done without pretence of deep feeling, not so much from the heart as from the intelligence, as if the mainspring of action were simply impatience at the intolerable stupidity which so generally characterizes our poor human attempts to be happy. Their attitude, in fact, to be seen on every page of Lady Mary's letters, is the attitude made classical in literature by the genius of Horace. "*Immortalia ne speres,*" "*frui paratis,*" and the rest, might have been the motto at the head of every sheet. Her philosophy of life, which she was for ever preaching in her old age, is just what Horace has put again and again with his incomparable felicity of phrase. " Nature has provided pleasures for every state," for old age and solitude, as well as for youth and society ; be moderate and temperate and contented ; prefer ease and simplicity to pleasure or ambition ; the small certainties of the present to the doubtful grandeurs or delights of the future ; train yourself to be superior to the universal folly of making life miserable by dwelling on woes that are either imaginary or inevitable. " *Quittez le long espoir et les vastes pensées* "; the path to happiness lies straight before you, if you will but see it, easy, smooth, and level ; it may not command any very romantic prospects, or promise any very interesting adventures; but such things, so far from being necessary, are undesirable and even dangerous, and, if you will climb steeper paths in search of them, you have only yourself to thank if the end of your journey is a broken neck.

She is, in fact, essentially, and more than anything else, a woman of intelligence. Or perhaps we have no word of our own which altogether covers the distinctive quality of her mind, for there is a life and brightness and, above all, a sure lightness of touch in her which are by no means the invariable possession of people whom we call intelligent.   Let us call her, as she is fairly entitled to be called, a *femme d'esprit.* That is what she actually is; what more she might have been, under more favourable conditions, it is hard to say.   No one who reads her letters can escape the feeling that nature meant her to play a larger part in the world.   It is clear that, wherever she went, she made an exceptional impression on those who met her.   Every page of her letters is the witness of a mind at once sane and acute in judgment and energetic in finding new interests and occupations for itself.   She can take the lead in society in London or Constantinople, and, with equal ease, she can live many years happy in herself and useful to her poorer neighbours in the solitude of an Italian country house.

"I did not think myself so considerable as I am," she writes on her arrival at Venice in 1739; "for I verily believe, if one of the pyramids of Egypt had travelled, it could not have been more followed; and if I had received all the visits that have been intended me, I should have stopped at least a year in every town I came through."

And yet what pleased her most on the

journey was, it seems, the Borromean Library at Milan, where she saw "several curious manuscripts." Evidently she was no ordinary woman, either in her tastes, or in the opinion other people held of her. And yet, in spite of ample means, good health, and a long life, she actually did very little. She exercised no political influence, and played no part in public life. Her verses are merely clever trifles. In fact her fame rests solely on these charming letters, for which we cannot be too grateful, but which, at the same time, leave us with a feeling that she was a woman who ought to have done something more. If only Mr. Wortley Montagu had been Sir Robert Walpole! One feels that she would then have had a real field for her powers. Her large endowment of "that uncommon thing called common sense" would have been invaluable in the political field, where the most useful qualification of a leader is, it has been said, to have more common sense than any man. The "town" and the wits were important in those days, and she was just the woman to manage them. And one may believe that, with the possession of a real opportunity, her ambition and the more serious side of her character would have been greatly stimulated. The

mental energy which, as it was, she concealed or diverted into the channel of light
reading, or threw into her letters to her
daughter, or expended in her garden, or
among her peasants, would, we may be
sure, have grown both in capacity and in
seriousness of aim if it had been allowed
a wider field. The frivolities and follies to
which she felt herself not merely confined
but almost in duty bound, in her actual
circumstances, would certainly have then
occupied far less of her time, or only sub-
served higher objects. It is evident that
she herself felt the cramped position in
which, as a woman, she was in that day
necessarily placed. Not that she ever says
so. It was the fashion in her day to affect
to have no serious interest in anything. She
did not begin it, as the story of Voltaire's
visit to Congreve shows: nor did it end
with her, as every one knows who has
suffered under Horace Walpole's tiresome
protestations that the only things he really
cared for in life were gossip and getting up
late in the morning. And she had more
cause than they had, for as a woman she
was doubly expected to decline the honour
of being thought to have a head on her
shoulders. Anyhow, it is certain that
she does, again and again, declare her

preference for trash and trifles, over matters of more serious interest :

"I am reading an idle tale, not expecting wit or truth in it, and am very glad it is not metaphysics to puzzle my judgment, or history to mislead my opinion." "I desire no other intelligence from my friends but tea-table chat." "I am as fond of baubles as ever, and am so far from being ashamed of it, it is a taste I endeavour to keep up with all the art I am mistress of."

But, perhaps, one may read her more genuine feeling in her constantly reiterated advice to Lady Bute to encourage her daughters in a taste for reading. She knew how much she owed to it herself, and was determined that it should not be her fault if her granddaughters were deprived of that surest and most unfailing of all sources of happiness.

"I know, by experience," she tells Lady Bute, "that it is in the power of study not only to make solitude tolerable, but agreeable. I have now lived almost seven years in a stricter retirement than yours in the Isle of Bute, and can assure you I have never had half an hour heavy on my hands for want of something to do. Whoever will cultivate their own mind will find full employment."

It is true that she adds the warning that the object of a girl's studies should be not reputation but amusement :

"Teach them not to expect or desire any applause from it. Let their brothers shine, and let them content themselves with making their lives easier by it."

But she cannot help showing now and then that her chains did gall a little, for all her protestations. Here is a letter in which she discusses the question, and one cannot but feel that, while her acceptance of the "subjection of women" may easily be a mere piece of formal deference to custom and tradition, what she has to say on the other side could only have come from herself, and, as its indignant tone shows, from her heart as well as her head :   .

"I confess I have often been complimented, since I have been in Italy, on the books I have given the public. I used at first to deny it with some warmth ; but, finding I persuaded nobody, I have of late contented myself with laughing whenever I heard it mentioned, knowing the character of a learned woman is far from being ridiculous in this country, the greatest families being proud of having produced female writers ; and a Milanese lady being now professor of mathematics in the university of Bologna, invited thither by a most obliging letter, wrote by the present Pope, who desired her to accept of the chair, not as a recompense for her merit, but to do honour to a town which is under his protection. To say truth, there is no part of the world where our sex is treated with so much contempt as in England. I do not complain of men for having engrossed the government; in excluding us from all degrees of power, they preserve us from many fatigues, many dangers, and perhaps many crimes. The small proportion of authority that has fallen to my share (only over a few children and servants) has always been a burden, and never a pleasure, and I believe every one finds it so who acts from a maxim (I think an indispensable duty) that whoever is under my power is under my protection. Those who find a joy in inflicting hardships, and seeing objects of misery, may have other sensations; but I have always thought corrections, even when necessary, as painful to the giver as to the sufferer, and I am therefore very well satisfied with the state of subjection we are placed in; but I think it the highest injustice to be debarred the entertainment of my closet, and that the same studies which raise the character of a man should hurt that of a woman. We are educated in the grossest ignorance, and no art omitted to stifle our natural reason; if some few get above their nurses' instructions, our knowledge must rest concealed, and be as useless to the world as gold in the mine. I am now speaking according to our English notions, which may wear out, some ages hence, along with others equally absurd. It appears to me the strongest proof of a clear understanding in Longinus (in every light acknowledged one of the greatest men among the ancients) when I find him so far superior to vulgar prejudices as to choose his two examples of fine writing from a Jew (at that time the most despised people upon earth) and a woman. Our modern wits would be so far from quoting, they would scarce own they had read the works of such contemptible creatures, though, perhaps, they would condescend to steal from them, at the same time they declared they were below their notice. This subject is apt to run away with me; I will trouble you with no more of it."

There is visible enough here, as I said, behind all disclaimers, the just and inevitable impatience of a clever woman at the contemptible position assigned to her sex; and this letter is not the only one, nor this the only subject, which exhibits Lady Mary with the temper of a reformer, likely to have anticipated the triumph of some modern ideas, if she had ever had the opportunity. Her friendship, too, with Mary Astell, the defender of women's rights in that day, is another indication in the same direction. No doubt her cool common sense would have saved her from the extravagances in which later advocates of the education of women have indulged. All she pleads for is equality of opportunity. As for equality of capacity, the politely imagined fiction of to-day, her clear head and happy turn for seeing things as they really are, would never have allowed her to be the dupe of any such absurdity. The claim that women should have the same liberty as men have to cultivate their minds, exercise and enrich their imaginations, and, in a word, aim at the perfection of every faculty they possess, is one thing: and whether urged on the ground of the happiness of the women themselves, or that of the men with whom they may live, or based on utility to the state, or on natural and indefeasible right, it is obviously plain sense and plain justice, and must before long be universally admitted. The assertion that the average woman is equal in ability to the average man is quite another thing, and one which unprejudiced people, who keep their eyes and ears open, will not be induced, even by the undoubted fact that very brilliant women, and very dull men, exist, have existed before, and will again, to regard as anything but a strange delusion, opposed to the experience both of the past and the present.

The only occasion on which Lady Mary occupied anything like a public position, was when she accompanied her husband on his embassy to Constantinople. That is one of the leading dates of her life, and as there are but a few of them, the rest may as well be given here with it. She was born in 1689, and was the daughter of Evelyn Pierrepoint, fifth Earl of Kingston, who was created Marquis of Dorchester in 1706, and Duke of Kingston in 1715. She had two remarkable grandmothers, and her mother was Lady Mary Fielding, through whom she was second cousin to the author of "Tom Jones." Passionately fond of reading, she managed to give herself an excellent education, and his attainments in classical studies are supposed to have been part of the attraction of Mr. Wortley Montagu, the friend of Addison, with whom, after a strange correspondence and court-ship, she eloped in 1712. He was a member of several Parliaments, and in 1716 was appointed Ambassador to the Porte. Lady Mary went with him, but they only stayed about a year, returning in 1718. She went abroad again in July 1739, and lived in different places, but principally at houses of her own at Brescia and Venice, till the end of 1761, when matters of business arising from her husband's death necessi-tated her return. They had never met since she left England, but had maintained a frequent and affectionate correspondence. She died a few months after her return in August 1762, leaving one son, Edward, whose eccentricities and vices were a per-petual source of annoyance to his father and mother. He died, leaving no issue, in 1776, having, it is said, become first a Roman Catholic and afterwards a Maho-metan. Lady Mary's only other child was the daughter who was " the passion of her life," Lady Bute.

There is nothing, it is clear, in Lady Mary's life that was specially likely to arouse the interest of a fully occupied posterity. Birth, marriage, and death are the chief events in it as they are in the lives of most of the sons and daughters of Adam. What attracts us in her is evidently not her life but herself.

There was, however, as has been said, one occasion on which she came, to some extent, before the eye of the public. She lived for a short time at Constantinople as the wife of the British Ambassador, and it was by letters describing her experiences during her husband's embassy that she first became known to a wider circle than that of her own acquaintance. They appeared in three volumes, a few months after her death. There is a good deal of mystery about the circumstances of their publication, as well as that of an additional volume which appeared in 1767. Mr. Moy Thomas, Lady Mary's most recent editor, seems to have proved that the fourth volume was a forgery, probably by John Cleland; and that the letters in the earlier volumes were not originally written as letters, but were prepared by Lady

Mary from a diary kept while she was abroad.

Under these circumstances, they cannot of course appeal to us as genuine letters actually sent to the people to whom they are addressed, appeal. Fictitious letters or speeches may be as fine or finer than real ones. They may even interest us as much, but the interest cannot be the same. Half the charm of letters lies in the inter-relation of two personalities. The letters to one friend differ from those to another, and while we are acquiring pleasant glimpses of a score of men and women, we are gaining the surest insight into the character of him or her whom we see under so many different aspects.

An interest of this sort these "Embassy" letters cannot have. But they have one of their own. They are, in the first place, delightful proof of Lady Mary's literary gift. Until perfect ease and perfect clearness, intelligence, vigour, and a touch of wit are found in combination much more often than they are at present, no collection of English classics will be complete in which the name of Lady Mary Wortley Montagu does not occur. And there is another thing. They are probably unrivalled as a picture of contemporary manners and customs in the parts of Europe Lady Mary visited. There is an obvious reason for this. They are the result of a rare, if not unique, combination. There were plenty of accounts of Turkey, as Lady Mary herself often remarks, but they were written by merchants or ordinary travellers, who had no opportunity of seeing anything but the externals of Turkish life. Lady Mary's position was a key that opened all doors. She could dine with the wife of the Grand Vizier, a Sultan's widow, spend an afternoon with the lovely Fatima, whose husband possessed the power of which the Vizier enjoyed the name, or stay some weeks in the house of a rich and learned Effendi. And then, with rare opportunities she combined an equally rare capacity to use them. Of the fifty or five hundred Englishwomen of the time, any one of whose husbands might have been sent to the Embassy at Constantinople, there was only one who could have written these letters. They contain a hundred interesting pictures of social habits in Austria and in Turkey, just as the letters of her later life do of those of Italy. For a history of European manners in the eighteenth century her three or four. volumes of letters would be in fact a document of first-rate authority in the field they cover. Some things she sees which few others would have had the chance of seeing, many which few beside her could have described as she has described them. A few of her statements and criticisms are of serious importance for the student of serious things like politics and morals; many are extremely amusing; more still are simply and delightfully curious. Here is a passage which may serve as a warning to that numerous class of intelligent people who in their impatience with the noisy squabbles of democracies are inclined to cast back longing eyes on the happy days of absolute princes and passive obedience:

"'Tis impossible not to observe the difference between the free towns and those under the government of absolute princes, as all the little sovereigns of Germany are. In the first, there appears an air of commerce and plenty. The streets are well built, and full of people, neatly and plainly dressed. The shops loaded with merchandise and the commonalty clean and cheerful. In the other, a sort of shabby finery, a number of dirty people of quality tawdered out; narrow nasty streets out of repair, wretchedly thin of inhabitants, and above half of the common sort asking alms."

One can imagine the satisfaction with

which Lady Mary, a Whig of the Whigs
by birth, marriage, temper, and conviction, would record this edifying contrast,
and point its most just and necessary
moral. And here is a letter which must
have given as much gratification to the
common sense of the woman as that did
to the political orthodoxy of the Whig.
We English have always taken up a
somewhat profane attitude towards the
mysterious sanctities of German etiquette,
and Lady Mary's invariable impatience
with all sorts and conditions of dull ways
and people was not likely to make her
more tolerant of these absurdities than
the rest of us. Here is her account of
Ratisbon:

" You know that all the nobility of·this place are
envoys from different states. Here are a great
number of them, and they might pass their time
agreeably enough, if they were less delicate on the
point of ceremony. But, instead of joining in the
design of making the town as pleasant to one
another as they can, and improving their little
societies, they amuse themselves no other way than
with perpetual quarrels, which they take care to
eternise, by leaving them to their successors ; and
an envoy to Ratisbon receives, regularly, half a
dozen quarrels among the perquisites of his
employment.
You may be sure the ladies are not wanting,
on their side, in cherishing and improving these

important *piques*, which divide the town almost into as many parties as there are families, and they choose rather to suffer the mortification of sitting almost alone on their assembly nights, than to recede one jot from their pretensions. I have not been here above a week, and yet I have heard from almost every one of them the whole history of their wrongs, and dreadful complaints of the injustice of their neighbours, in hopes to draw me to their party. But I think it very prudent to remain neuter, though, if I was to stay among them, there would be no possibility of continuing so, their quarrels running so high, they will not be civil to those that visit their adversaries. The foundation of these everlasting disputes turns entirely upon place, and the title of Excellency, which they all pretend to ; and, what is very hard, will give it to nobody. For my part, I could not forbear advising them (for the public good) to give the title of Excellency to everybody, which would include receiving it from everybody ; but the very mention of such a dishonourable peace was received with as much indignation as Mrs. Blackacre did the notion of a reference ; and I began to think myself ill-natured, to offer to take from them in a town where there are so few diversions, so entertaining an amusement."

She has many amusing things to say of Vienna, some of which cannot decently be stolen from her pages. She tells us of "the natural ugliness with which God Almighty has been pleased to endow" the ladies of the Court, and the unnatural edifices "covering some acres

of ground" with which they adorn it;
their more than Ratisbonian sense of their
own importance, so that on an occasion
when two coaches met in a narrow street
at night,

" the ladies in them, not being able to adjust the
ceremonial of which should go back, sat there with
equal gallantry till two in the morning, and were
both so fully determined to die upon the spot rather
than yield in a point of that importance, that the
street would never have been cleared till their
deaths, if the emperor had not sent his guards to
part them ; and even then they refused to stir, till
the expedient was found of taking them both out in
chairs exactly at the same moment ; after which it
was with some difficulty the *pas* was decided between
the two coachmen, no less tenacious of their rank
than the ladies."

Another curious fashion, very comfort-
ing to ladies of a certain age, is that the
beauties there are twenty years older than
in London.

" I know you cannot easily figure to yourself a
young fellow of five-and-twenty ogling my Lady
Suffolk with passion, or pressing to lead the
Countess of Oxford from an opera. But such are
the sights I see every day, and I don't perceive
anybody surprised at them but myself. A woman
till five-and-thirty is only looked upon as a raw girl,
and can possibly make no noise in the world till
about forty. I don't know what your ladyship may
think of this matter ; but 'tis a considerable comfort
to me, to know that there is upon earth such a

paradise for old women; and I am content to be insignificant at present, in the design of returning when I am fit to appear nowhere else. I cannot help lamenting upon this occasion the pitiful case of too many good English ladies, long since retired to prudery and ratafia, whom if their stars had luckily conducted hither, would still shine in the first rank of beauties:"

which last sentence, one must remark, is not alone in showing that Lady Mary, learned as she was in many foreign tongues, had not chosen to resign her woman's privilege of doing as she pleased with the grammar of her own.

For Turkey and the Turks she has little but praise. She seems to have enjoyed her stay amongst them immensely. She had opportunities of seeing many curious things, amongst them the fair Fatima, the wife of the Grand Vizier's lieutenant, "whose beauty effaced everything that has ever been called lovely either in England or Germany," and the virtuous Sultana Hafitan, who still spent several days each week in tears for a husband who had been dead fifteen years, but who at least had the consolation of occasional magnificence: for she received Lady Mary in a dress so loaded with diamonds and emeralds and pearls that her guest put its value at a hundred thousand pounds;

and she gave her an " extremely tedious " dinner of fifty dishes : but its magnificence equalled that of her dress.

" The knives were of gold, the hafts set with diamonds. But the piece of luxury that grieved my eyes was the tablecloth and napkins, which were all tiffany, embroidered with silks and gold, in the finest manner, in natural flowers. It was with the utmost regret that I made use of these costly napkins, as finely wrought as the finest handker-chiefs that ever came out of this country. You may be sure that they were entirely spoiled before dinner was over. The sherbet (which is the liquor they drink at meals) was served in china bowls; but the covers and salvers massy gold. After dinner, water was brought in a gold basin, and towels of the same kind as the napkins, which I very unwillingly wiped my hands upon ; and coffee was served in china, with gold *soucoupes*."

But she had more serious occupation than dining with Sultanas. " I study very hard," she tells Pope : we find her comparing what she sees around her with the descriptions of Theocritus, and noting, as she reads Pope's " Homer," that the Homeric manners were by no means extinct.

" The princesses and great ladies pass their time at their looms, embroidering veils and robes, sur-rounded by their maids, which are always very numerous, in the same manner as we find Andro-mache and Helen described."

She copies inscriptions, and makes " a

collection of Greek medals," thereby astonishing the antiquaries, who

"stare in my face when I enquire about them, as if nobody was permitted to seek after medals till they were grown a piece of antiquity themselves."

Reading of various kinds occupied a great deal of her time, and in the week's diary she gives in one of her letters, three of the days are put down as spent in reading, one being given to the classics, one to English, and one to the study of Turkish, in which she describes herself as already very learned, sending proofs of her proficiency in the shape of translations of Turkish love poetry. Foreign languages, indeed, by choice or by necessity, occupied her so much that she declares herself in danger of losing her English, and one cannot be surprised considering that she was living, as she says,

"in a place that very well represents the tower of Babel: in Pera they speak Turkish, Greek, Hebrew, Armenian, Arabic, Persian, Russian, Slavonian, Wallachian, German, Dutch, French, English, Italian, Hungarian; and, what is worse, there are ten of these languages spoken in my own family. My grooms are Arabs; my footmen French, English, and Germans; my nurse an Armenian; my housemaids Russians; half a dozen other servants Greeks; my steward an Italian; my janissaries Turks."

Turkish institutions find a by no means severe critic in her. The slaves, she asserts, are no worse off than domestic servants elsewhere, and the Turkish ladies, far from being the objects of pity they are usually stated to be, are, in Lady Mary's opinion, the freest and most fortunate in the world. She has a great deal to say in support of this view: and confirms it by an account of a Spanish lady of her acquaintance, who, after having been captured by a Turkish admiral, refused the offer of a ransom, and became his wife, and, on his death, the wife of his successor.

Lady Mary, however, did not cease to be an Englishwoman and a Whig, because she found the Turks to be in some matters by no means so bad as they were painted. She kept her compliments for their social institutions: their political system, with a Sultan at once a despot and a slave, a lawless soldiery, and a peasantry exposed to constant plunder, persecution and even murder, was as odious and intolerable in her eyes as in those of any other person of common honesty and common sense. She first of all lets her indignation have free play on the subject ; and then she uses the Turk, just as she had used the German

Residenz Stadt, to point the proper Whig moral, and reduce the Tories to confusion.

"I cannot help wishing, in the loyalty of my heart, that the parliament would send hither a ship-load of your passive-obedient men, that they might see arbitrary government in its clearest, strongest light, where it is hard to judge whether the prince, people, or ministers, are most miserable."

But interesting as these letters from Vienna and Constantinople are, they have not the attraction possessed by the later letters which were written from Italy to Lady Bute. And the reason is simple. All Lady Mary's letters show us the clever woman of the world; these alone show us also the devoted and affectionate mother. The others, too, are mainly occupied with the people she met and the sights she saw; but from her Italian solitude she could have but one subject, the best of all, herself. Ten letters from her Brescian farm tell us more about her than all the three volumes from Constantinople; and, what is more, make us like her far better. For it is just that side of her which is least attractive which gets emphasized when she is living in the world of London, Vienna, or even of Venice; but here, in her country retirement, these things seem a long way off, and the lines, which fashion and society had cut so deep in her character, are worn almost smooth by solitude and age, and by simpler and healthier occupations, so that they no longer produce more than a rare and faint impression. The picture of her and of her life which we can put together from this long series of letters to her daughter is a fairly complete one. We see her " resisting all invitations," while " reading, writing, riding and walking " find her full employment ; sometimes quite wrapped up in her land and her crops, so that, as she tells her daughter in the words of some old song—

> " All my whole care
> Is my farming affair,
> To make my corn grow and my apple-trees bear "—

from which she not only derives great pleasure, but " so much profit that, if I could live a hundred years longer, I should certainly provide for all my grandchildren "; sometimes spending weeks entirely alone, and then again having her solitude relieved or disturbed by such alarming distinctions as the quite unexpected visit of a princess, attended by her grand master, a cardinal's brother, as well as by ladies, pages, guards, and " a long et cetera of inferior servants ";

or another, even more embarrassing, when,
according to " the way of living in this province," which is " what I believe it is now
in the sociable part of Scotland, and was
in England a hundred years ago," thirty
ladies and gentleman, on horseback, with
their servants, suddenly appeared " with
the kind intent of staying at least a fortnight, though I had never seen any of
them before." However, after being enter-
tained with poultry and fiddles, as the
princess had been with sack posset and
piquet, they, too, were got rid of, although
much disappointed at not being pressed
to stay, " it being the fashion to go in
troops to one another's houses, hunting
and dancing together a month in each
castle." But these were only magnificent episodes in her life ; as a rule, the
days passed quietly enough. Here is a
delightful letter, which describes her
Brescian " dairy-house," and the life she
lived in it : -

"I have been these six weeks, and still am, at
my dairy-house, which joins to my garden. I
believe I have already told you it is a long mile
from the castle, which is situate in the midst of a
very large village, and has not vacant ground
enough about it to make a garden, which is my
greatest amusement, it being now troublesome to
walk, or even go in the chaise, till the evening.

I have fitted up in this farmhouse a room for myself—that is to say, strewed the floor with rushes, covered the chimney with moss and branches, and adorned the room with basins of earthenware (which is made here to great perfection) filled with flowers, and put in some straw chairs and a couch-bed, which is my whole furniture. This spot of ground is so beautiful, I am afraid you will scarce credit the description, which, however, I assure you shall be very literal, without any embellishment from imagination. It is on a bank, forming a kind of peninsula, raised from the river Oglio fifty feet, to which you may descend by easy stairs cut in the turf, and either take the air on the river, which is as large as the Thames at Richmond, or by walking in an avenue two hundred yards on the side of it, you find a wood of a hundred acres, which was already cut into walks and ridings when I took it. I have only added fifteen bowers in different views, with seats of turf. . . . I am now writing in one of these arbours, which is so thickly shaded the sun is not troublesome, even at noon. Another is on the side of the river, where I have made a camp kitchen, that I may take the fish, dress, and eat it immediately, and at the same time see the barks, which ascend or descend every day from Mantua, Guastalla, or Pont de Vie. This little wood is carpeted, in their succeeding seasons, with violets and strawberries, inhabited by a nation of nightingales, and filled with game of all kinds."

This was her paradise ; and here is her manner of life in it, "as regular," she says,

"as that of any monastery. I generally rise at six, and, as soon as I have breakfasted, put myself at the head of my weeder women, and work with them till nine. I then inspect my dairy and take a turn among my poultry, which is a very large inquiry. I have, at present, two hundred chickens, besides turkeys, geese, ducks, and peacocks. All things have hitherto prospered under my care; my bees and silkworms are doubled, and I am told that, without accidents, my capital will be so in two years' time. At eleven o'clock I retire to my books: I dare not indulge myself in that pleasure above an hour. At twelve I constantly dine, and sleep after dinner till about three. I then send for some of my old priests, and either play at picquet or whist till 'tis cool enough to go out. One evening I walk in my wood, where I often sup, take the air on horseback the next, and go on the water the third. The fishery of this part of the river belongs to me; and my fisherman's little boat (where I have a green lute-string awning) serves me for a barge."

This letter, for purposes of quotation, is indeed what Lady Mary calls it, "of unconscionable length," but it is worth giving for the fulness of its picture of her home, and of the life she lived in it. It is a quiet harmless existence, peaceful and serene, as if all life were a summer's evening. The most striking thing about it is the abundance of resources, and the astonishing activity of interests, which she must have possessed in herself to enable her to continue it so long. Perhaps it was not so idle as she paints it; for, though she often declares that she attains " what has long been the utmost of her ambition " in " whiling away an idle life with great tranquillity," she will, nevertheless, tell us elsewhere that she does

" what good I am able in the village round me, which is a very large one; and have had so much success, that I am thought a great physician, and should be esteemed a saint if I went to mass."

Indeed she did so much for her neighbours that they were determined to erect a statue of her, and were only prevented by her refusing to give sittings to the sculptor, and telling them her religion would not permit it.

" I seriously believe," she says, " it would have been worshipped, when I was forgotten, under the name of some saint or other, since I was to have been represented with a book in my hand, which would have passed for a proof of canonisation. This compliment was certainly founded on reasons not unlike those that first framed goddesses, I mean being useful to them, in which I am second to Ceres. If it be true she taught the art of sowing wheat, it is sure I have learned them to make bread, in which they continued in the same ignorance Misson complains of. I have introduced French rolls, custards, minced pies, and plum-pudding, which they are very fond of. 'Tis impossible to bring them to conform to sillabub, which is so unnatural a mixture in their eyes, they are even shocked to see me eat it; but I expect immortality from the science of butter-making, in which they are become so skilful from my instructions, I can assure you here is as good as in any part of Great Britain."

From all which it is plain that her life was neither wholly idle nor wholly selfish, for here is the best possible evidence of her usefulness, the supreme proof positive of spontaneous gratitude. And so these twenty-two years of voluntary exile glided away in easy and kindly contentment. They were not all spent on the Brescian farm ; for besides her two houses there, we find her occupying palaces at Lovere and at Padua, and a house in Venice, to say nothing of the magnificent palace of Cosmo dei Medici on the lake of Garda, which she hired for a time, and describes as finer than any royal palace in Germany, France, or England, a place of oranges and pomegranates, baths and fishponds, fountains and cascades and marble gods and goddesses. But wherever she goes, the picture we get of her is the same ; she is everywhere what she calls herself, that " uncommon kind of creature, an old woman without superstition, peevishness, or censoriousness." With ample means, good hearing sight and memory, "appetite enough to relish what I eat," and "sound uninterrupted sleep " ; a taste for two of the purest of human pleasures, for gardening which took her into the air, and for reading which kept her happy indoors at

Padua for some hours a day, and makes
her say that "if relays of eyes were to be
hired like posthorses," she would "admit
none but silent companions"; gifted, too,
from her birth with good sense and good
temper, and "a certain sprightly folly"
that made her always take things, as far
as possible, on their bright side, she ought
to have been a happy woman; and she was.
Happy in the past, in the present, and
even in the future, she will amuse herself
by telling Lady Bute of promising young
men who might do for the granddaughters
she had never seen; though she, indeed,
would not live to see the wedding:

"I no more expect to arrive at the age of the
Duchess of Marlborough than to that of Methusalem;
neither do I desire it. I have long thought myself
useless to the world. I have seen one generation
pass away; and it is gone; for I think there are
very few of those left that flourished in my youth.
You will perhaps call these melancholy reflections:
they are not so. There is a quiet after the abandon-
ing of pursuits, something like the rest that follows
a laborious day. I tell you this for your comfort.
It was formerly a terrifying view to me that I should
one day be an old woman. I now find that Nature
has provided pleasures for every state. Those are
only unhappy who will not be contented with what
she gives, but strive to break through her laws, by
affecting a perpetuity of youth, which appears to
me as little desirable at present as the babies do to
you, that were the delight of your infancy. I am

at the end of my paper, which shortens the sermon of, dear child, your most affectionate mother."

The letters to Lady Bute are her best, and that for two reasons. Frank and easy as the others are, as all she wrote was, these are something more : they are ease and spontaneity itself. But it is not only that. It is that in them, and in them almost alone, she shows us all that was in her heart. Her daughter was the passion of her life; the one being, it seems, for whom she ever felt the love that brings with it a necessity for constant intercourse of one kind or another, a sense of impatience and anxiety at its failure or interruption. She was a kind mistress, a sincere friend, a loyal, even an affectionate wife; but there never was any one in the world who could have given her a sleepless night except the daughter, who was, as it were, her mother's only child, and seems, too, to have been all that a mother's heart could ask an only child to be.

That is Lady Mary's weak point. There is too much head in her, and too little heart. Her impulses and emotions are always in leading-strings to the cool common sense which is her dominant characteristic. She was evidently very much in love with her husband, enough to be willing to leave everything for him, or, as she says, to " part with anything for you but you "; but Cupid had no bandages that could blind her eyes; and she is astonishingly frank as to her own feelings and his, and in the expressions of her doubts about the probability of their getting on together very long in a country retirement. Even with her daughter she will have no false sentiment, and amusingly declines gratitude on her part for having brought her into the world, on the ground that " there was a mutual necessity on us both to part at that time, and no obligation on either side." Everywhere she is for the bare fact, exactly as it is, with no emotional or imaginative illusions about it, preferring prudence to heroism, tranquillity to fame, the clear-sighted common sense which, to quote her own example, gave Atticus riches and security, to the splendid dreams which were as fatal as they were glorious to Cicero.

It is not a very inspiring creed, whatever else may be said in its favour. Man is not really set in motion by sugar-plums, Carlyle declared : and certainly no calculation of hedonistic profit and loss, however brilliant and infallible, ever came near to touching his heart,

But we must not quarrel with Lady Mary, who was, after all, but a woman of her day. Besides, it is we who are in her debt, not she in ours. Only she must not ask us to pay her in coin, which, for her, we simply have not got. She has given us much pleasure and some profit, too, perhaps: we can offer in return, and very gladly and sincerely, praise, admiration, even gratitude: but there is one thing which we cannot promise her—the thing which every letter in her many volumes assures afresh to Madame de Sévigné—a place in our hearts.

SWIFT.[1]

THE common conception of the character of Swift has done him less justice than has been accorded to most of the *Dii majores* of English prose and poetry. Popular impressions can never include details; but so long as Addison, for instance, is thought of as a kind of personified *mitis sapientia*, Johnson as a unique compound of rather rough-handed and hard-hitting honesty, sense, and humour, Keats as an embodiment of an almost effeminate sensitiveness to beauty in all its forms, so long justice, even if she cannot be said to have reached her perfect work, attains as much of it as can be demanded of human weakness. But this can be hardly said in Swift's case. The

[1] Swift's Letters occupy the last five volumes of " The Works of Jonathan Swift, D.D., with Notes and a Life of the Author, by Sir Walter Scott, Bart."; nineteen volumes, Constable, 1824. There is also an edition of his " Letters and Journals," selected and edited by Mr. Stanley Lane Poole, and a new edition of his " Prose Works " is in course of publication, of which the first volume, with an introduction by Mr. Lecky, appeared in 1891. There is an interesting picture of Swift in Mrs. Woods' novel, " Esther Vanhomrigh."

picture which rises before the ordinary eye at the mention of his name is one of a man of almost unparalleled pride and insolence, hating and despising all around him, and uttering his hatred with an unchecked brutality, which knew no pleasure so great as that of trampling on the hopes or affections of others. No one will pretend that there is nothing of this in Swift; but it is strange and cruel, that nothing else in him should have strength enough, after the vicissitudes of a hundred and fifty years or more, to assert its right to a place in the popular judgment about him. With this feeling one is very glad, after a study of the letters has filled one with a sense of the great injustice done to Swift, to find on taking up some of his most recent critics that they are conscious of it, and anxious to repair it: Mr. Churton Collins, for instance, in his " Biographical Study," and Mr. Lane Poole, who says in the preface to his excellent " Selection," " I am confident that no one can read these letters without materially changing, if he ever held it, the traditional view of Swift as a morose cynic." Happily, it is, on the whole, the true and not the false conception of a great man which generally survives; and even in Swift's case, it is probably not yet too late to hope that the larger and juster estimate which is formed by those who have made the effort to know what manner of man he really was may find its way out of that narrower circle, and establish itself as the final thought about him throughout the nation, among whose great names his has an undying place.

The cause of the injustice done him is not far to seek. His own cynical whim of parading his hates and hiding his loves laid a foundation, which the unexplained dislike of Johnson, the literary dictator of the last half of the eighteenth century, and the natural and inevitable dislike of the typical Whig Macaulay, who succeeded for a time in our own century to something like Johnson's authority, confirmed and completed. It is curious that Johnson, who carried his combative churchmanship so far as to declare (under provocation, of course) that Episcopalians in Scotland were "as Christians in Turkey," should not have had a friendlier feeling for the man who cared more for the Church perhaps than any one who has played a considerable part in English politics between Laud's day and Mr. Gladstone's. Yet, if I were bound to suggest an explanation of the fact, I think it would be in

this very direction, in the quarter where
they seem to meet so closely, that I should
look for the cause of divergence. On such
questions as the respect due to the clergy,
and the disrespect due to Presbyterians,
Swift and Johnson were, indeed, as one
and the same man. But go a little deeper
and it is not so. The whole cast of Johnson's mind and character was deeply
impressed, perhaps more than that of any
writer of equal eminence, with the pro-
foundest sense at once of the truth and
the mystery of the Christian religion. He
was for ever dwelling on the tremendous
questions which that religion raises, and to
some of which it gives answers; answers
which he reverently accepted. And it was
not only the speculative side of religion
which moved him so greatly. The idea of
duty was as constantly present to him as
that of faith. His diary, his private prayers,
his conversations with Boswell and others
remain to prove him a man possessed with
a very exceptional craving after what can
hardly be given a less name than personal
holiness. There is nothing of this in
Swift. He was perfectly loyal to the
doctrines of his church, but there is not a
sign of his having ever thought about
them seriously in Johnson's way as the

greatest and most important of all materials for meditation. His piety was perfectly sincere, but, compared with that of Johnson, it gives the impression of a mood which returned on stated and official occasions, instead of an essential and principal part of the man, colouring every act and thought of his life. It is not easy to pass behind Swift's curtain of cynicism, but I should say that anything like Johnson's deep sense of sin, and personal dependence upon the help of God in daily life, was quite alien to his nature. That fine but melancholy saying of Johnson, for instance, " the better a man is the more afraid is he of death, having a clearer view of infinite purity " belongs, whatever its truth or falsity, to a realm of thought far above any reach of such a man as Swift. The higher possibilities by which man transcends this world of sense, were known to Johnson only on the side of religion : they were not known to Swift at all. Dryden's " Cousin Swift, you will never be a poet " was a true saying. And poetry and religion are alike in this, that they must both know how to see " the light that never was on sea or land." It was not in Swift's nature to do that. No one ever had his eyes more intently and invariably fixed on the things before him at his feet. He was a plain man alike in practice and in speculation, and his genius consisted simply in a very unusual capacity for clear seeing and plain speaking. A thousand feelings of reverence and awe would have made it impossible for Johnson to write the "Tale of a Tub"; and it is, I suspect, just in this fundamental difference between the two men that the origin of Johnson's dislike is to be looked for. Nothing moved his anger like profanity, and it is likely enough that he never forgave what he would regard as profanity of the worst kind, the profanity of a clergyman.

If Johnson's dislike for Swift may be explained in this way, that of Macaulay needs no explanation. Macaulay was before all things a Whig, and Swift is hardly better known as the author of "Gulliver" than as the literary agent, one might almost say the executioner, of the brief triumph of the Tories. He is accordingly, for the Whig essayist, "the apostate politician, the ribald priest, the perjured lover, a heart burning with hatred against the whole human race, a mind stored with images from the dunghill and the lazarhouse." The full cruelty of such a picture as this, with all the shadows in poor Swift's character so mercilessly exaggerated, and all the relieving lights, which most certainly were to be found in it, so absolutely excluded, can only be realized by those who remember that, for good reasons or bad, the opinion of the average Englishman is simply that of Macaulay. Very probably, indeed, he is not acquainted with any other, and, if he is, Macaulay's directness and plainness and his habit of treating all questions as if they were so simple that the plainest of men could not go wrong about them, has given him an authority with the average man which overrides all criticism. Besides it is never to be forgotten that the average Englishman is a Whig, pure and unadulterated. The very secret of the long triumph of the Whigs is just that, that they so exactly understood the nature of their countrymen. The essence of Whiggery is the suppression of the imagination in politics. No sentimental loyalty towards the Stuarts, no reverent attachment to the ancient national Church, on the one hand, and, on the other, no " enthusiasm " after the manner of Whitfield in religion, no passionate first principles after the manner of Rousseau in politics—these are the characteristics of the true Whigs, and they are or have become so entirely a part of the middle class Englishman, that with the meteoric exceptions of Chatham and Disraeli, they may be said to have dominated our public men from 1688 to the present moment. The dislike of the House of Commons and the constituencies both of abstract reasoning and of appeals to the imagination has, in fact, become a commonplace; and when we indulge in an outburst either of loyalty or of patriotism, it is generally justified on purely business principles. By whatever name you call him, then, the common Englishman is a Whig. Not even Burke, attacking the French Revolution for its disregard of Whig legalities and decencies, nor Scott, half apologizing for the warmth of his love of Scotland, could afford to treat him as anything else. Swift himself, to the very end of his life, claimed to be "a zealous Whig," and, in essentials, no one ever was so more completely; for his whole attitude towards politics is that of the man of strong common sense, practical and businesslike, much more a hater of actual abuses than a stickler for any fine theories of what ought to be. Whatever the question in hand, Ireland, or the Church, or the disputes of Harley and Bolingbroke, all he asks is that men of sense and honesty should act in public affairs as they do with regard to their own. But his name has been identified with his brief moment of importance; and he is remembered in English tradition not as the pupil or prototype of the Whig reformers but as the friend and ally of Atterbury and Bolingbroke.

In this way, from a combination of unkind circumstances, no figure in our literary history has received harder measure than Swift. Those who take the trouble to read his letters will be surprised to find how widely the real man differs from the accepted portrait. He was neither hero nor saint, but to call him saint and hero would not be travelling so far from the truth in the one direction as Macaulay's invective does in the other. The " apostate politician " lived in days when party ties were very loosely defined. Whigs sat in the same cabinet with Tories, Tory ministers sought and obtained the support of moderate Whigs, and Swift, when he became a supporter of Harley and the new Government in 1710, turned his back on no principle he had previously professed, even if his impatience made him do less than justice to men whom he had till then highly honoured. The " ribald priest "

was loyal both to the creed and practice
of his Church, setting an example, even,
of careful performance of his ecclesiastical
duties, and treating his position at the
head of a cathedral as a trust to be con-
scientiously administered in the interests
of the Church. He was, like Pope, " of
the religion of Erasmus," and like Erasmus
was impatient of the abuses and the absurdities that have found their way into
ecclesiastical doctrine and discipline ; and,
though it is true that the absence in him
of the finer sense of spiritual things prevented his feeling, as a saintlier man would
have felt, that even the corruptions of
religion must be handled with some care
lest the ridicule intended for them be
carried on in the reader's mind by old
association, till it seem to strike at religion
itself, still that was an error of inadvert-
ence, and no one who knew him well, as
one may judge from Bolingbroke's letters,
could ever fancy that his " ribaldry," however unfortunate, proceeded from the doubt
or disloyalty of a man who was a priest
without being a Christian. There is again
no reason to think that he can, in any
strict sense of the words, be justly called
a " perjured lover" ; and there is the
clearest proof that the " heart burning

with hatred against the whole human race " was one which was for ever planning and carrying out the kindest and most generous projects for the benefit of men and women who had no claim on him. There is not an article in Macaulay's indictment for which there is not some colour; and it is just in that that the cruelty of it lies; for not only is there not one of them all which is not grossly exaggerated, there is only one, the last, which is not exaggerated so grossly that those who have seen anything of the real Swift may not pronounce it essentially libellous and untrue.

But let us pass from controversy and apologetics, and take a look at some of the habits and characteristics of the great Dean, as his letters reveal them. The central thing about him is his love of independence. No one could fail to be struck by this, of course, but, perhaps, the extreme point to which he carried it, and the way in which it dominated his whole life and character, has hardly received the notice it deserves. He was, perhaps, the most independent man who ever lived. This is a conspicuous trait even in his writings. There, as elsewhere, he followed his own path. The dominant notes

in the literature of his time were the turn
for moral and metaphysical speculations,
and the new " politeness " which Addison
introduced.   Swift was a man of the creed
and the ten commandments, and preferred
his own common sense to all the philosophy in the world.   His style, the most
vigorous and downright that ever was
written, is as far removed as anything can
be from the gracious urbanity of Addison.
But if he is independent, or rather self-
dependent, as an author, he is a hundred
times more so as a man.   Indeed, this
may be almost said to be the key to his
whole life.   It was for this, no doubt, at
least in part, that he would not make
Stella his acknowledged wife ; for this that
he scraped and hoarded, and for this, too,
that he liked to pay his hosts the value of
his dinner, and refused a gift of £50 from
Harley in a manner so unmistakable as
to prevent any further attempt of the kind.
It was for this, most conspicuously of all,
that he bullied dukes and lectured great
ladies, so that he could assure himself
that he was not surrendering to the seduc-
tive influences of rank and power.   For
the same reason again he would rather
stay in Ireland, " wretched dirty doghole "
as it is, " a place good enough to die in,"

than return to the society of Pope and
Gay and Bolingbroke, because there he is
at least "a freeman among slaves," and
the dignity of his Deanery "damps the
pertness of inferior puppies and squires,
which, without plenty and ease on your
side the Channel would break my heart in
a month." No doubt the same thing was
at the bottom of his quarrel with Sir
William Temple, another matter about
which Macaulay has given a very false
impression. He speaks of Swift as a
" humble menial " at Moor Park, and of
Stella as a waiting-maid in Sir William
Temple's servants' hall. Undoubtedly
they were both in a dependent position,
but language of this sort is most mis-
leading. Macaulay speaks as if Swift's
position had been little higher than that
of a footman, but gentlemen were no more
accustomed in the reign of William III.
than they are in that of Victoria to ask
their footmen to sit down to dinner with
them, still less to join with them in entertaining their sovereign. Swift did both
at Moor Park, and though it is true that
the only instance we have of his proud
spirit stooping to use the language of an
inferior is a letter to Sir William Temple,
and though he himself speaks of having

been " in pain " when Sir William Temple
looked "cold and out of humour," it
wants much more to prove that the relations between them were anything but
those so common in that day, of scholar
and patron.   Distinctions of rank were far
more marked then than now, and not only
the secretaries, but the cousins and even
the sons of a great man addressed him in
language which none but a servant would
employ to-day.   A great household two
hundred years ago was much larger than
those of to-day, and very often included
scholars, chaplains or relatives, who lived
" domestically," as Lord Ossory said of
Swift, but were in a totally different
position from those whom we now call
" domestics." Macaulay's mistake lies, in
fact, just in this, and he speaks of Swift
and Stella as if they had been domestics
in the modern sense : they were so only
in the older and larger application of the
word.   Swift's soreness did not arise from
being treated like a footman, which he was
not ; it arose from being unable to bear
being treated like a secretary, which he
was.   This fiery love of independence
remains the same throughout, and was at
once the pride and the torture of Swift's
life.   His is no solitary case, but there is

no instance more signal and striking of the fate attending genius which thinks to force its way, erect and unswerving either to right or left, through the multitudinous mass of inert obstruction which the world has ready to block its progress. When one thinks of Swift or Chatterton, the later rebel whose punishment was instant execution, the earlier who suffered the more cruel penalty of a lingering torture, one cannot but remember Bacon's saying about Nature, which seems at times so true also of the world, that she is only to be conquered by obedience. Happily in the case of the world, its truth is only partial ; for the most part of us, the needed lesson is rather of disobedience than of obedience. But for a temper like that of Chatterton, all made up of intractable pride and defiance, the most infinite possibilities of fame or power are lost or wasted simply for want of the knowledge that it is not so difficult to turn the world's flank, where it keeps no guard, but that those who insist on charging its front are dashed back and broken almost as surely as a wave against a wall of rock. It was the same with Swift. Whether we who live a hundred and fifty years after his death would have taken so much interest

in a suppler and more tactful Swift may
be doubtful enough; but it is certain that,
if he had had a little more of those
qualities in him, his great gifts, his sterling
honesty of purpose, his hatred of injustice
great or small, and his zeal for the public
good, would have found a larger sphere to
work in than could possibly be afforded by
the Deanery of St. Patrick's.   His impracticable arrogance does not, indeed, seem
to have deprived him of any of his intimate
friends : they, no doubt, knew him well
enough to make allowances; but it must
have greatly stood in his way with others.
" That parson knows enough who knows a
lord," says Cowper, in one of his Satires,
and that was as true in Swift's day as in
his.   But then the parson must always
remember that a lord is still a lord though
he deigns to know a parson, and that was
what never once occurred to Swift.   He
has a saying himself, hatched, of course,
in his Deanery, when he had risen above
the heads of his brethren, that " parsons
are not such bad company, especially
when they are under subjection."   But
who was less under subjection than he?   It
was probably not particularly agreeable to
the Duchess of Ormond to have a clergyman whom nobody had known a few years

before taking strange liberties in her drawing-room, and if she forgave it, we may be
sure that there were others to envy and
detest the upstart. The Duchess of
Shrewsbury probably thought that an
invitation from her was a thing to be
accepted, not one to be played with : the
Duke of Beaufort and Lord Keeper Har-
court can hardly have been pleased to
have been kept out of the first dining club
of the day through the influence of a man
who had neither birth, nor wealth, nor
official position. The whole court was
slighted by his open refusal to dine in any
but the selectest company, or even sometimes in any but of his own choosing;
and his answer to Bolingbroke, who
showed him his bill of fare to tempt him
to dinner, " Poh ! I value not your bill of
fare ; give me your bill of company,"
however well it passed as a *bon mot* can
hardly have added to his popularity.
Success is largely an affair of the liking
of those who know a man a little, and it
is not surprising that Swift, who cannot
have been much liked outside the immediate circle of his intimates, never
succeeded in climbing beyond a Deanery.

It is a pity for all reasons that he did
not. No doubt he was not qualified to be

a spiritual force in the church, but there would have been nothing conspicuous in that. What he was qualified to do, and would most undoubtedly have done, was to resist all jobbery wherever his influence extended, and promote everywhere men of ability and character. If he had been made a Bishop, his diocese would in ten years have been the best manned in the kingdom. As it was, all through his life there was nothing more at his heart than the promotion of men worth promoting.

" This I think I am bound to," he says, "in honour and conscience, to use all my little credit towards helping forward men of worth in the world."

" There is scarcely a man of genius of the age who was not indebted to him," says Mr. Lecky in his introduction to the useful new edition of the "Prose Works." He made his club of lords and ministers come to the help of poor authors, and did what he could for them himself: and in later years when he wrote from St. Patrick's to Viceroys and other great personages it was usually on behalf of some neglected man of worth. English public life was never so corrupt as in his day. Bribery and the back stairs made the appointments in church and state alike, but Swift, so far as his influence went, was a splendid exception to all this. He declares, in a letter to Lady Betty Germain, that, in all the requests he had made to the Duke of Dorset, the Irish Lord Lieutenant, he had had in view the Duke's own honour.

"I have very few friends in want. I have kindred enough, but not a grain of merit among them, except one female, who is the only cousin I suffer to see me. When I had credit for some years at court, I provided for above fifty people in both kingdoms, of which not one was a relation. I have neither followers, nor fosterers, nor dependers: so that if I lived now among the great, they might be sure I would never be a solicitor, out of any regard but merit and virtue: and in that case, I would reckon I was doing them the best service in my power: and if they were good for anything I would expect their thanks."

He would not, indeed, allow Pope to call him a patriot, or Pulteney to honour him as a "Philanthropus"; but for all his declarations that he hates men more than toads and vipers, and that Pope has more virtue in an hour than he in seven years, never were patriotism and philanthropy more brave and genuine. His powerful pen saved Ireland from a few abuses, and would have saved her from the rest if statesmen had had the sense to listen to him and the honesty to do as he told them. His work for Ireland was the only thing he did in all his life for which he received fair pay. That at least brought him honour and popularity. He had "a thousand hats and blessings" as he walked the streets of Dublin: Lord Carteret says that "orders fulminated from the sovereignty of St. Patrick's" were always strictly obeyed. Walpole was warned that it would need an army to arrest him: and when a dissenting lawyer, whom he had ridiculed, threatened vengeance, thirty noblemen and gentlemen "waited upon the Dean in form and presented a paper, subscribed with their names, in which they solemnly engaged to defend his person and fortune, as the friend and benefactor of his country." No man was ever more indignant at abuses, and his indignation found plenty of matter to exercise itself upon in Ireland. Long before, in his London days, he wrote to Stella:

"I dislike a million of things in the course of public affairs: and if I were to stay here much longer, I am sure I should ruin myself with endeavouring to mend them."

And things were far worse in Ireland.

"This kingdom is now absolutely starving," he tells Pope in 1735, "by the means of every oppression that can be inflicted upon mankind—shall I not visit for these things? saith the Lord. You advise me right, not to trouble myself about the world, but oppression tortures me."

He did what he could, with his opportunities great and small: used an interview with Walpole, not in getting anything for himself, but in letting the minister hear some unpleasantly plain truths about Irish grievances; talked sense to a series of Lords Lieutenant; prevented some jobs at Trinity College, such as the attempt of the Fellows to get the professorships limited to themselves; used all his influence against " oppression by landlords," insisting that the rents should be such that the tenants should be able to live in a tolerable manner; and wrote to Sir John Stanley on behalf of one of his tenants, telling him " You neither must nor shall act as an Irish racking squire," while promising at the same time that if he had been misinformed, he would "drive your tenant out of doors whenever he presumes to open his lips again to me on any occasion."

That was the man, for ever trying to put the world a little to rights, and declaring all the while that it was an abominable world, past praying for and not worth

an effort of any kind. It is this last trait
that contributes the most telling things
to be found in his letters, his flashes
of hatred and contempt for knaves and
fools. They are not, indeed, so delightful
as Johnson's outbreaks at the expense
of "bottomless Whigs" and "odious
wenches," because they leave a taste of
bitter seriousness in the mouth, while
every one can hear Johnson's laugh behind
his growl. In Swift it is the burden of the
Psalmist, "they are all gone out of the way,
they are altogether become abominable,"
uttered with an explosive indignation
which makes one think of Landor or
Carlyle. Still vigour is an attractive
quality in literature, and Swift's is of the
fieriest. To one gentleman, who failed to
pay rents due to St. Patrick's, he first
gave a lecture on his want not only of
Christianity, but of such pagan virtues as
honour and justice, and then remarked,
with refreshing candour, " If you resent
anything I have said, it will much lessen
the credit of your understanding." To
another, who had infringed upon some
land which he had added to the glebe of
his living at Laracor, " as an encourage-
ment to a clergyman to reside among you
whenever any of your posterity shall be

able to distinguish a man from a beast,"
he says with equal frankness:

"From the badness of your education and the
cast of your nature, I expected nothing from you
that became a gentleman; and from the practice of
lording over a few Irish wretches, and the natural
want of better thinking, I was sure your answer
would be extremely rude and stupid, full of very
bad language in all senses:"

and concludes:

"I have ordered a copy of this letter to be taken,
with an intention to print it as a mark of my esteem:
which, however, perhaps I shall not pursue, for I
could willingly excuse our two names from standing
in the same paper, since I am confident you have as
little desire of fame as I have to give it you."

When a friend of his was about to
settle in the county Kilkenny, he wrote to
him an account of its sloughs and thieves
and beggars, and added:

"I demand that you shall not relish one bit of
victuals, or drop of drink, or the company of any
human creature within thirty miles round Knock-
togher, and then I shall begin to have a tolerable
opinion of your understanding."

He dismissed a footman without a
character, who, after other faults, had
behaved unkindly to a poor woman: and

when the man returned and begged a character of some sort, the Dean wrote:

"Whereas the bearer served me the space of one year, during which time he was an idler and a drunkard, I then discharged him as such; but how far his having been five years at sea may have mended his manners, I leave to the penetration of those who may hereafter choose to employ him:"

on which flattering testimonial Pope took him into his service, where he stayed till Pope died. He can combine brevity with his vigour, as in his advice to Vanessa: "Settle your affairs and quit this scoundrel island"; or his description of a young lady who is "goggle-eyed and looks like a fool"; or, again, of the Bishop of Ossory: "the silliest, best-natured wretch breathing, of *as little consequence as an egg-shell.*" The man whose contempt for his fellows finds its expression in a humorous touch like that could have had no bad heart at bottom. And of the charm which he exercised, the warm affection he aroused, the feelings of Pope and Arbuthnot, of Harley and Bolingbroke, to say nothing of those of Stella and Vanessa, are witness enough. Nor did he receive affection only without returning it. His relations with Stella and Vanessa were indeed falsified by something which must remain a mystery, and both Stella, whose long deferred, merely nominal and entirely secret marriage was a poor satisfaction of her claims on him, and Vanessa, whose passion he ought never to have allowed and enjoyed, as he did not return it, had all the right in the world to complain of his conduct. It is certain that he loved Stella, and equally certain that he did not wish to marry her. The least unlikely explanation of what is not fully explicable is that, for some reason, he could not think of marriage, and forgot, as men have done before and since, that the fact that such an idea never entered his mind was no safeguard against its entering those of others. To the end he was determined that no one should know of his marriage, and succeeded so well that we cannot be said to know it now. Even when in an agony about Stella, dreading the death of "the fairest soul in all the world," and calling it "the greatest event that can ever happen to me," he does not forget to take precautions against her dying in the Deanery. Yet he loved her as few men love : there is a world of passion, or of affection as strong as passion, behind the famous "Only a woman's hair."

But that is an old story, the best known

as well as the least understood thing about
Swift. His affection for his friends has
been less remembered. It is as much to
his honour as the other, even after all
allowances have been made, is to his
lasting dishonour. To Pope, "my dearest,
almost only constant friend," he is always
the same. He wants him to come and live
for awhile at the Dublin Deanery, while
Pope is anxious that Swift should settle
altogether at the Twickenham Villa. Their
language to each other never changes :
"may God always protect you and preserve
you long"; "pray God reward you for your
kind prayers ; I believe your prayers will
do me more good than those of all the
prelates in both kingdoms "; " you are
the best and kindest friend in the world,
and I know nobody, alive or dead, to
whom I am so much obliged."   That is
Swift's tone to Pope ; and Pope's to Swift,
except for the silly mystification about the
publication of his letters, is just the same,
and, I believe, at bottom, almost as entirely
sincere, though its expression has that
taste of the man of letters about it which
belongs to everything Pope wrote.

"Let this, however, be an opportunity of telling
you—What ?—what I can tell : the kindness I
bear you, the affection I feel for you, the hearty

wishes I form for you, my prayers for your health of body and mind, or (the best softenings of the want of either) quiet and resignation. You lose little by not hearing such things as this idle and base generation has to tell you: you lose not much by forgetting most of what now passes in it. . . . If the evil of the day be not intolerable (though sufficient, God knows, at any period of life), we may, at least we should, nay we must (whether patiently or impatiently), bear it and make the best of what we cannot make better, but may make worse. To hear that this is your situation and your temper, and that peace attends you at home, and one or two true friends who are tender about you, would be a great ease to me to know and to know from your-self. . . . My dear Dean, whom I never will forget or think of with coolness, many are yet living here who frequently mention you with affection and respect. Lord Orrery, Lord Bathurst, Lord Bolingbroke, Lord Oxford, Lord Masham, Lewis, Mrs. P. Blount, allow one woman to the list, for she is as constant to old friendships as any man. And many young men there are, nay, all that are any credit to this age, who love you unknown, who kindle at your fire, and learn by your genius. Nothing of you can die, nothing of you can decay, nothing of you can suffer, nothing of you can be obscured, or locked up from esteem and admiration, except what is at the Deanery: just as much of you only as God made mortal. May the rest of you (which is all) be as happy hereafter as honest men may expect, and need not doubt, while (knowing nothing more) they know that their Maker is merciful! Adieu!"

No one who could write so well as this could fail to be aware of it and enjoy it; but it is a mistake to think that Pope was insincere because he makes literature of his private feelings. He was a born man of letters, and for whatever purpose he took up his pen, was incapable of forgetting for a moment to give to what he had to say the most telling or beautiful form he could command.

Swift says, in his poem on his own death :

> " Poor Pope will grieve a month, and Gay
> A week and Arbuthnot a day."

This is rather unjust to Arbuthnot, but it marks very well the greater seriousness of the friendship between Swift and Pope as compared with that which he maintained with Gay.

When Swift writes to Gay he is chiefly occupied in telling him to " learn to value a shilling," and remember that " a whole thousand pounds brings you but half-a-crown a day," advice which Gay needed, since, as Swift puts it, " Providence never designed him to be above two-and-twenty." But he felt a real sense of loss at Gay's death, and showed it in many ways, not least characteristically by his support of Pope against Gay's sisters : " I had rather the two sisters were hanged, than to see his works swelled by any loss of credit to his memory." And that magnanimity, which was such a conspicuous part of his character, showed itself as much in his friendships as in other matters: as was seen in 1714, when both his great friends were summoning him to come to them and he unhesitatingly preferred the task of consoling the fallen Harley to the pleasures and possibilities of sharing the triumph of the victorious Bolingbroke. But it is not merely with his intimates that the real affectionateness of his disposition comes out. When an insignificant writer, one Harrison, for whom Swift had got a place, lay dying, he got money together for his assistance at once, and went with Parnell to give it to him. "I was afraid to knock at the door: my mind misgave me." The servant tells him his master is dead. "Think what grief this is to me! I went to his mother and have been ordering things for his funeral. . . . I could not dine with Lord-Treasurer, nor anywhere else: but got a bit of meat toward evening. No loss ever grieved me so much; poor creature!"

When the Duke of Hamilton was killed in the famous duel, Swift hurried to the Duchess and stayed with her two hours. "I never saw so melancholy a scene— she has moved my very soul." This is

Macaulay's " heart burning with hatred against the whole human race!"

It has lately been remarked that old-fashioned people of good manners never talked of health or money, while we talk of nothing else. I am afraid the bad habit is older than Sir Algernon West allowed. Perhaps Swift began it; his letters at any rate are full of both. We hear incessantly of the walks he took for health's sake, ten miles a day, twelve, even fifteen sometimes; of the ill effects of the Lord-Treasurer's wine; of his inability nevertheless to do without wine, two pints a day; of his liking for fruit and fear of eating it; of his " sad vulgar appetite," which " cannot endure above one dish "; of his giddinesses and fits of illness ever more and more serious as time goes on. As for money, it is everywhere, from the journal to Stella to the last letters that left the Deanery. His economy has an eye for small things as well as great; he grudges the shillings for coaches and chairs; wishes he had his half-crowns back when Harley's porter dies; complains of knaves who " make huge void spaces " in the Deanery cellars; and is for ever saving and urging Pope and Gay and Sheridan to save. Yet he gives away

more than £100 a year, it seems, out of
an income not very large, was a generous
benefactor to many humble friends all
through his life, and had his final
charity in view as at least one object of
his saving. The other was the old feeling:
"you know," Mrs. Woods makes him
say in "Esther Vanhomrigh," "the thing
I save by my parsimony, though I write
it in pounds, shillings, and pence, is
in truth my independence." "I can live
upon £50 a year," he told Bolingbroke,
"but I cannot endure that *otium* should
be *sine dignitate*." He will not allow Gay
to count himself rich enough "till you are
worth £7,000, which will bring you £300
per annum, and this will maintain you,
and when you are old will afford you a
pint of port at night, two servants, and an
old maid, a little garden, and pen and ink."
"Wealth is liberty, and liberty is a blessing fittest for a philosopher." No doubt
he gives it, as he admits, a rather large
interpretation. His conception of the
necessary "*subsidia senectuti*," which he is
always saying he cannot do without, does
not stop at "books in large print and an
honest parson," nor at three horses and
two servants, which belong, he considers,
to his condition of "*ambitiosa paupertas*";

he goes further, declaring that "valetudi-
narians must live where they can command, and scold : I must have horses to
ride; I must go to bed and rise when I
please, and live where all mortals are sub-
servient to me. I must talk nonsense when
I please, and all who are present must com-
mend it." It is a dreary picture of old age
which he sends Pope with his invitation :
the solitary bachelor, securing his comfort
as his only substitute for a lost or impossible happiness, by the presence of
"a race of orderly elderly people of both
sexes, who are of no consequence, and
have gifts proper for attending us."

Would he have had a happier life if he
had never received that commission from
the Irish Bishops about the First-fruits,
and never seen Harley or Bolingbroke?
Did those famous years in London destroy
the germ of a happy, peaceful, useful
Vicar of Laracor? Could that restless
spirit have lost its restlessness and grown
content with willows and canals and
cabbages out of doors, and books and
parsons "who play backgammon" within?
Probably not. Probably the malady, or
the fiery force of brain and will which
produced it, could only have been lulled
to sleep by opiates more potent than any

that were to be found at Laracor. Yet he turns affectionately to the thought of his Irish home in the midst of all his business and importance.

"O, that we were at Laracor this fine day! The willows begin to peep, and the quicks to bud. . . . I would fain know whether the floods were ever so high as to get over the holly bank or the river walk; if so, then all my pikes are gone; but I hope not. Why do you not ask Parvisol these things, sirrahs? And then my canal, and trouts, and whether the bottom be fine and clear?"

He loved exercise, too, and the open air, noting that it is "delicate walking weather" one day in January, 1711, when Rosamond's Pond (in St. James's Park) is "full of the rabble sliding and with skates (if you know what they are)." But the taste for simple pleasures is of all things the soonest killed by ambition, and a few years at the centre of politics, as perhaps the most influential commoner in England, made it impossible for him to rest satisfied either in a study or a garden. No occupations, indeed, demand more patience than those of the student and the gardener, and Swift's was a temperament which nature had not made very patient, and illness and disappointment had rendered ever less and less so. The man, who himself declared that a

burning sense of wrong, "*saeva indignatio,*"
was the central characteristic of his
nature, was not likely to be a great
writer of letters.   That art of the Epi-
cureans lies as much out of the reach of
cynic bitterness as it does out of that of
Stoic strenuousness.   The ease which
only just escapes idleness, the good-nature
which borders on weakness, the love of
little things which does not forget to
honour great things, a wide-wandering
curiosity, simple affections, and simple
pleasures, a hopeful willingness to let the
eye rest always, as far as may be, on the
bright and beautiful places which even an
imperfect world produces in plenty—those,
and not great thoughts or great passions,
are the gifts which make a Cowper or an
Edward FitzGerald.   There is too much
tension, intellectual as well as moral, in
Swift for him to be of this company.   He
is for ever pressing on in fiery haste
towards some goal of ambition attained,
or benevolence accomplished, or denun-
ciation uttered and driven home.   He
cannot loiter on his way and pluck the
flowers ; and it is only so that epistolary
flowers can be plucked.   The very unity
of all he wrote — one of his greatest
literary merits — is really fatal to his

letters. They hardly ever wander or play, and that is what letters must do if they would be perfect.

There is, indeed, something of these qualities in that unique document, the journal to Stella:

"Is that tobacco at the top of the paper, or what? I do not remember I slobbered. Lord, I dreamed of Stella, &c., so confusedly last night, and that we saw Dean Bolton and Sterne go into a shop; and she bid me call them to her, and they proved to be two parsons I knew not; and I walked without till she was shifting, and such stuff, mixed with much melancholy and uneasiness, and things not as they should be, and I know not how; and it is now an ugly gloomy morning. At night, Mr. Addison and I dined with Ned Southwell, and walked in the park; and at the coffee-house I found a letter from the Bishop of Clogher, and a packet from MD. (*i.e.*, Stella and Mrs. Dingley). I opened the Bishop's letter and put up MD.'s, and visited a lady just come to town, and am now got into bed, and going to open your little letter, and God send I may find MD. well, and happy, and merry, and that they love Presto as they do fires. O, I will not open it yet! yes, I will! no, I will not; I am going; I cannot stay till I turn over; what shall I do? my fingers itch; and I now have it in my left hand; and now I will open it this very moment."

This is the very genius of sincerity, and here and elsewhere in the journal, Swift seems to have, as no one else has ever had, that capacity for putting everything

of every kind on paper, which is of all the
gifts the most essential perhaps to the
writer of letters.　Indeed, as a plain tale,
told with astonishing realism and wealth
of detail, the journal has few or no rivals.
But there is a breathlessness about its
very realism which injures it as a series
of letters.　It wants atmosphere, a certain
grace of utterance, a greater variety of
mood.　And in the later letters from the
Deanery, there is the same monotony,
without the same fulness of self-revelation.　He never confessed himself to
any one as he had done to Stella.　And
after her death, his trifling, always apt to
take the form of mock abuse, of which the
modern reader soon grows tired, grows
ever rarer and less pleasing, as he sinks
into age and decay and the final insanity.
Thus the letters are only first-rate here
and there.　But of course there are first-
rate things to be found in them, which
tempt quotation.　Who, for instance, can
willingly pass over Swift's story of Bede,
who loads the Irish with praises for their
piety, learning and innumerable virtues,
and then " overthrows them all, by
lamenting that, alas! they kept Easter
at a wrong time of the year ! "

How are we to judge him as we look

back on him ?   Not as the worst of men certainly, nor as the best.   A character with grave faults about it, it is clear, but such as were so much caused by even graver misfortunes that one scarcely knows how to blame him for them ; a brain ready, active, eager as few have been, living always in the practical and the present, giving even to the adventures of Gulliver the strangest air of every-day fact and reality ; a man of immense possibilities, whether as a literary force or as a political, of which only a small part were realized.   Fate was unkind to him and unkind to the world in confining him to St. Patrick's.   He was born to rule something larger than a deanery, and would not have disgraced a greater station than any the Church had to offer. One would gladly have seen that masterful nature, which used its small mastery with such rare public spirit, placed in a wider sphere ; one cannot but fancy, that if by some strange fortune things had been so, all that pent-up energy and care for the public interest would have found happy exercise, the rulers of Europe would have had a bright example set before them, and some happy nation cherished the memory of a " Patriot King."

JOHNSON.[1]

PERHAPS the only excuse for writing about Johnson is that one cannot help it. If English men of letters, or that wider class who read, but do not write, were polled to-morrow for the choice of a man, whom they would like to pass the evening in talking about, Johnson would probably get twice as many votes as any one else. The reasons are obvious and on the surface of things. There is no one whom we know so well—that is one and perhaps the most important. Then the racy vigour of his talk, its Gargantuan abundance and humour, its occasional brilliance of wit, the " alarums and excursions " in which it never had an equal, and the serious interest which is always underneath to give them all their value, leave on the dullest company, which has Johnson for its subject, an impression that the evening has been one in which every one has

[1] Johnson's Letters are to be found in the " Letters of Samuel Johnson, LL.D., collected and edited by George Birkbeck Hill," in two volumes, Clarendon Press, 1892.

shone. He has all our patriotism, too, not to say our patriotic prejudices, in his favour, for he is as incontestably the most absolutely English among our men of letters as Falstaff is among the characters they have created for us. Johnson and Falstaff together, indeed, give us the typical Englishman, not all that is highest in our race, perhaps, nor all that is lowest, but all that is universal and essential. It is notable, for instance, that some of the things which have most distinguished us among the nations, our poetry for one, are not conspicuous in the typical Englishman at all, any more than they are in Falstaff or Johnson. But the reason of reasons why Johnson is the only conversational dish of which no properly constituted palate can ever tire lies, of course, in the cook who served him up—in the delightful, incomparable Boswell, most genuine of hero-worshippers and prince of biographers, who, while he lived, was, we easily believe, the " man whom everybody likes," who " never left a house without leaving a wish for his return," and to whom, a hundred years after his death, we owe a debt of gratitude incalculably beyond any chance of repayment.

And if, for all these reasons, we may

and must talk about Johnson, why, after all, may we not write about him too? There are no discoveries to be made about him, perhaps, and it is not necessary to aim at making any; but surely a talk about old friends and favourites is just as lawful on paper as it is by the fireside. No man of sense, indeed, would occupy himself with writing about books, if he were confined to sifting the new ones, of which the great majority must perforce be of little value, and never allowed to talk of the old ones, where the sifting has been long done, and there is nothing more to do but to enjoy.

Still it is not exactly the old road, so often traversed, which I propose to take with a view to seeing Johnson once more. Our route is not so frequented, and, indeed, does not deserve to be; but though it cannot rival the attractions of the other, it too will show us some very fine points of view as we go along, and though we may prefer to return by the other, it will be strange if we do not admit that the new one, which is shorter, too, than the old, was well worth seeing at least once in our lives. We are to see Johnson as he shows himself in his Letters, rather than as the master of showmen exhibits him in

the Life. We will not, indeed, bind
ourselves by any self-denying ordinance
which would absolutely forbid a side
glance now and then at Boswell and the
Mitre, or the Western Highlands. "A
vow is a horrible thing," as Johnson has
told us himself, and of all the vows impossible of accomplishment, which weak
man has ever made and broken, the
most hopeless and unnecessary would be
one that bound us to keep clear of Boswell when talking of Johnson. The two
must go down the ages together; what
Boswell has joined no one need ever waste
his pains in trying to separate. But it is
the letters that we are especially to keep
before us: the letters which Dr. Birkbeck
Hill has got together for us with a loyalty
and industry fit and graceful in a member
of Johnson's own College, and of which
the University of Oxford, honouring
Johnson now as it honoured him and was
honoured by him in his lifetime, has with
equal fitness undertaken the publication.
In Oxford, at least, the memory of Johnson must remain always green. It is true
he never lived there long; but he was
always a frequent visitor, a loyal and
grateful son, a source of just pride, to
the University which had given him

the degree he had been unable through
poverty to claim.   And there is another
link in the fact that the practice and appreciation of the kind of talk in which
Johnson has no equal has lingered longer
at the Universities than anywhere else.
" Taverns " are deserted, and clubs are
become hotels in which strangers glare at
each other ; but the Oxford and Cambridge common rooms still exist, however much reduced by married fellowships.
And there, if anywhere, is heard the talk
that Johnson loved. For no one can read
Boswell without discovering that Johnson
did not care to talk about just anything.
It is true that he once said " There is
nothing, Sir, too little for so little a
creature as man " ; but that was not the
principle on which he talked. His subjects were books and men, as a scholar's
should be ; and whatever paradoxes he
threw out by the way, his serious interest
in what is most serious in literature and
in man is never hidden for a moment.
The sallies which we quote and hope never
to forget owe half their flavour to the fact
that they come from one of the wisest
and most thoughtful men who ever lived.
And his thought is, above all, of morals.
It is especially from that point of view

that he looks both at literature and life. And in that lies another link with the Universities, especially with Oxford, where the love of letters has always and avowedly aimed at being what the Stoic philosopher said it should be, a preparation for life. In fact, the mind of Johnson was exactly what that of Oxford has always been. There is not a figure in the whole roll of English letters who shared so fully, realized indeed, one may almost say, so exactly, the Oxford ideal of a union between sound learning and true religion.

Nothing, then, could be more fit than that the world should receive the first collected edition of Johnson's Letters at the hands of an Oxford editor, with the aid of the resources of the Oxford Press. And one may be sure that every Oxford man worthy of the name will follow the completion of the great edifice which Dr. Birkbeck Hill has been so long engaged in raising to the honour of Johnson, with interest and good wishes as warm as those with which the greatest of recent Oxford figures, "*ipse Johnsonianissimus*," followed its first instalment, the edition of Boswell. As long as Jowett lived, only his friends knew how good a right he had to that title, and to the dedication which gave it to him: we all know it now, since his biographers have shown him to us confessing " I have read it fifty times."   Nor can we be at all surprised, for he too possessed the Oxford love of letters and the Oxford seriousness, though not quite in the traditional form; and he had besides the sense of humour in which the love of Boswell is finally made perfect. Perhaps, if the life of every Oxford man who cares for books at all were written, though that would indeed be a serious price to pay for the discovery, we might arrive at some astonishing disclosures as to the number of those who have worshipped at the Johnsonian shrine with the same fervour and frequency as Jowett.

But to come to the letters.   Dr. Birkbeck Hill is justified in saying that they have been a little too much overshadowed by the talk.   It is inevitable, but it is unjust.   Johnson is not, indeed, a born letter-writer.   He wrote unwillingly always, sluggishly often, formally, almost pompously, sometimes.   Lightness of touch was the last gift he could claim.   It is not present even in his talk, where all other good things were met together.   It is still rarer in his letters, and it is, as we have seen, the very secret of the letter-writer's art. Johnson, indeed, never in his life either said or wrote anything that was not interesting in substance. But his manner is too often that of the preacher or the pedagogue; always a wise preacher, certainly, and always a sensible pedagogue; but a letter is neither a sermon nor a lecture. One cannot but think with a sigh now and then of the spontaneity of Madame de Sévigné, the " free-and-easiness " of Fitz-Gerald, the learning and good taste which are so delightfully united in Gray, the humour and simplicity which make the charm of Cowper. But after all a writer, whatever he writes, can have no greater merit than that of always talking sense. Of that nothing can deprive Johnson. His natural bent and early circumstances were not in favour of the cultivation of life's lighter graces, and, in spite of the famous compliment to Mrs. Siddons, we smile at his " Sir, I count myself a very polite man." Letters certainly ought to have just these qualities, which Johnson lacks—we will make no attempt to deny it—and the fact keeps Johnson out of the first class of letter-writers. But forget for a moment to be too strict in insisting on all our epistolary rights; forget Cowper and Gray and FitzGerald; think rather of literature as a whole than of the epistolary species of it; and the letters of Johnson rank at once among the things that deserve to be read. Literature is the record of what the human brain has thought wisely, or nobly imagined. It is great literature according to the degree of adequacy with which it records the depth and subtlety of thought, the loftiness and elusive beauty of imagination. Johnson had little imagination; in his case we are not concerned with that side of literature; but, in his special way, he is one of the masters of thought, and no man's thought was ever better seconded by his tongue and pen. His written language is sometimes called clumsy, but that is a complete mistake. It is turgid, pompous, heavy, if you will; but there is never a doubt of its doing the work he meant it to do. He uses an axe, perhaps, where a penknife would be enough; but his axe cuts as clean as another man's penknife. There is one advantage, too, amid many disadvantages, which his pen has over his tongue. He often said what he did not mean: in his writings, from " Rasselas " to the letters to Mrs. Thrale, we never have anything but what he really thought. Malicious people might use

parts of his talk to prove that he was a
bully and a boor: from his letters none
could pretend to gain any impression but
that of a man to whom religion, faith, and
duty were ever-present realities, a man of
warm heart and great kindliness, of rare
vigour and acuteness of intellect, of an
unfailing common sense almost equally
rare. A large part of their interest lies,
indeed, as always in the case of letters,
in the revelation of himself which they
unconsciously make. Take, for instance,
those that he wrote to that too typical
eighteenth century clergyman, his friend
Dr. Taylor. Their defects are on the
surface. If it had been Cowper or Fitz-
Gerald who had stayed at Ashbourne, we
should have known all the little ways of
the place. There would have been something to correspond to the "quarterdeck"
at Little Grange and the garden at
Weston; we should have had glimpses
of the daily meals, when they dined and
what they ate, sketches of the neighbours,
stories of the very servants. As it is,
almost the only thing we have of the kind
is the famous bull. We do not so much
as know whether Dr. Taylor wore a smart
wig, or one like that of his great guest.
Did he play cards? Did he read? Or

did he find incessant plotting after further
preferment a sufficient occupation for the
day ?   How did Johnson get through the
day when staying there ?   One gathers
that he did not enjoy himself very much,
but for the rest "we do not know," "we do
not know" is the only answer to all such
questions.   We get more information from
Boswell's two visits to the house than
from all the letters Johnson dated from
it.   Boswell stayed there only twelve days
altogether, but they produced for us not
only plenty of talk, but a few pretty details
like the "large roomy postchaise, drawn
by four stout, plump horses and two
steady, jolly postilions," which Boswell
considered "an equipage properly suited
to a wealthy, well beneficed clergyman";
the "crystal lustre or chandelier," which
Johnson would not have lighted in honour
of his birthday, and the "large and
luminous" church; besides such delightful pictures as those of Johnson using
a long pole to clear dead cats and other
obstructions out of Taylor's waterfall (the
same by which he once sat reading the
Enchiridion of Erasmus); of Boswell
and Johnson talking in the garden at
night; of Boswell at the inn, the "Green
Man," whose mistress was "a mighty

civil gentlewoman," and gave him an engraving of her sign. Johnson writes scores of letters either to Dr. Taylor or from his house; but little as we know or could expect to learn of Ashbourne life from Boswell, we learn even less from Johnson. That Dr. Taylor lived on milk, though Johnson frequently advised him to "drink a great deal" of wine; that in 1770 Ashbourne was "a very pleasant house, with a lawn and a lake, and twenty deer and five fawns upon the lawn"; that in 1777 the Doctor was "all for cattle, and minds very little either does or ·hens," being "very busy getting a bull to his cow and a dog to his bitches"; that "Mr. Chaplin of Lincolnshire" gave him £126 for one of his cows: this is almost all the list of little things to be got out of his letters. The famous bull is too big to be mentioned among little things, but he lives chiefly as having been no doubt the great cause of Johnson's complaint that Taylor's talk was of bullocks, and as having given occasion to Johnson's humorous comment on the man who came to apply for a farm, was taken to see the bull and said that he had seen a bigger: "Do you think he is likely to get the farm?"

In all these letters there is no scene like that of Johnson clearing out the waterfall, no chance sketch like Boswell's "mighty civil gentlewoman" at the "Green Man." Nor is the little we do get to be gathered from the letters to Taylor, which contain hardly any allusions of the kind. And yet, though far from Johnson's best, they have a real interest of their own. They are the picture of a wise man advising a man who was anything but wise ; of a man of strong common sense, who had known real trouble, trying to shame a rich grumbler out of losing life and health in imaginary woes. Johnson was the most loyal of friends. He and Taylor had little in common, but they had known each other all their lives, and their friendship had become, as he put it, "valuable for its antiquity." Taylor might be uneasily conscious, as Johnson thought, that a man so strict as Johnson must disapprove of his unclerical habits ; but whatever there was of good in the pluralist Prebend of Westminster must have had a sense of the possession of a bulwark of strength in Johnson's wisdom, goodness and unalterable affection. Here is a letter which is proof of all three :

" You have no great title to a very speedy
answer, yet I did not intend to have delayed so
long. . . . There is one honest reason why those
things are most subject to delays which we most
desire to do. What we think of importance we wish
to do well, to do anything well requires time, and
what requires time commonly finds us too idle or
too busy to undertake it. To be idle is not the best
excuse, though if a man studies his own reforma-
tion it is the best reason he can allege to himself,
both because it is commonly true, and because it
contains no fallacy ; for every man that thinks he is
idle condemns himself and has therefore a chance
to endeavour amendment, but the busy mortal has
often his own commendation, even when his very
business is the consequence of Idleness, when he
engages himself in trifles only to put the thoughts
of more important duties out of his mind, or to
gain an excuse to his own heart for omitting them.

" I am glad, however, that while you forgot me
you were gaining upon the affections of other people.

" It is in your power to be very useful as a
neighbour, a magistrate, and a Clergyman ; and he
that is useful must conduct his life very impru-
dently not to be beloved. . . .

" When you come to town let us contrive to see
one another more frequently, at least once a week.
We have both lived long enough to bury many
friends, and have therefore learned to set a value
on those who are left. Neither of us now can find
many whom he has known so long as we have
known each other. Do not let us lose our intimacy
at a time when we ought rather to think of increasing it. We both stand almost single in the world :
I have no brother, and with your sister you have
little correspondence. But if you will take my advice, you will make some overtures of reconciliation

to her. If you have been to blame, you know it is your duty first to seek a renewal of kindness. If she has been faulty, you have an opportunity to exercise the virtue of forgiveness. You must consider that of her faults and follies no very great part is her own. Much has been the consequence of her education, and part may be imputed to the neglect with which you have sometimes treated her. Had you endeavoured to gain her kindness and her confidence, you would have had more influence over her. I hope that before I shall see you she will have had a visit or a letter from you. The longer you delay the more you will sometime repent. When I am musing alone, I feel a pang for every moment that any human being has by my peevishness or obstinacy spent in uneasiness. I know not how I have fallen upon this; I had no thought of it when I began the letter, (yet) am glad that I have written it.

> "I am, dearest Sir,
> "Your most affectionate,
> "SAM: JOHNSON."

A superficial criticism may call such a letter dull; but when had dulness so much sense and matter? How subtle and true is the distinction between the man who confesses idleness, and the man who alleges business as a reason for leaving things undone! How affectionate the plea for closer friendship! How full of the wisdom of charity, what he says about the sister; how full of the most real conviction of duty and responsibility, of a goodness based on something far deeper than any mere good-nature, those last words about himself!

This is, perhaps, Johnson's longest letter to Taylor; and it gives us the most serious side of their friendship. He generally wrote more briefly and less intimately. The affection is still there, though not so conspicuous; and so is the good advice, but it seems to come from the head almost as much as from the heart. There is as much contempt of muddle as love of the muddler in it.

"I do not wonder that Mr. Woodcock is somewhat incredulous when you tell him that you do not know your own income; pray take care to get information, and either grow wiser or conceal your weakness."

Or again;

"you are the first man who, being able to read and write, had packets of domestick quarrels made by a servant. Idleness in such a degree must end in slavery."

Or once more;

"let your servant be as treacherous as you suppose, it is your own fault if she has anything to betray. Do your own business, and keep your own secrets, and you may bid defiance to servants and to treachery."

When Taylor's wife ran away from him he was inclined to mope in the country, and shrank from his annual residence at

Westminster. Johnson gave him bracing advice :

"That your mind should be harried and your spirits weakened, it is no wonder; your whole care now should be to settle and repair them. To this end I would have you make use of all diversions, sports of the field abroad, improvement of your estate or little schemes of building, and pleasing books at home ; or if you cannot compose yourself to read, a continual succession of easy company. . . . Be always busy.

"You will hardly be at rest till you have talked yourself out to some friend or other, and I think you and I might contrive some retreat for part of the summer where we might spend some time quietly together. . . .

"I hear you talk of letting your house at Westminster. Why should you let it? Do not show yourself either intimidated or ashamed. . . . Your low spirits have given you bad counsel. You shall not give your wife, nor your wife's friends, the triumph of driving you out of life. If you betray yourself, who can support you ? "

But Taylor could make himself miserable without such good reason as a runaway wife ; and he is always in need of a tonic from his friend. It always came in practical shape :

"I hope you are diligent to take as much exercise as you can bear. I had rather you rode twice a day than tired yourself in the morning. I take the true definition of exercise to be labour without weariness. . . . Sadness only multiplies self. Let us do our duty and be cheerful." "Bustle about your hay and your cattle, and keep yourself busy with such things as give you little solicitude." "Be particularly careful now to drink enough." "Do not muse by yourself; do not suffer yourself to be an hour without something to do. Suffer nothing disagreeable to approach you after dinner."

This last, perhaps, savours rather of the counsel of perfection; unless it be, as some will think, suggestive merely of an elderly gentleman's post-prandial nap. But the rest is sound and sensible enough, and probably did as much for Taylor as advice was capable of doing. The whole of the correspondence, indeed, bears witness to Johnson's loyalty and helpfulness as a friend.

There is, however, another which does so to a still greater degree, and is besides more interesting in itself, as addressed to a more interesting man. Perhaps Boswell's character owed almost as much to Johnson as Johnson's fame has owed to Boswell. He was only twenty-two on that May afternoon when he was sitting after tea with Davies, the bookseller, and Johnson's "awful approach" was announced to him. Who shall say how things might have turned out with him if Johnson and hero-worship had not arrived just at the critical moment to balance the weakness and vanity, the temptations to

the bottle and things more dangerous
than the bottle, which were certainly in
his character, and not likely to be at their
weakest at twenty-two?

Johnson wrote and talked all his life
with an avowed wish to do all the good
he could.　Wherever his voice or his pen
could penetrate, people were obliged to
think of life as a serious thing.　No doubt,
in one way or the other, he influenced
hundreds, perhaps thousands; but there
is no one in whom we can follow his
influence as we can with Boswell.　Of
course the soil was ready, or he could
not have sown the seed; but if he had
not sown it, it is likely enough that it
would never have grown anything but
weeds.　Reverence was the quality that
saved Boswell.　You see it in his constant
attitude towards religion, towards the
very places and buildings in which it has
made a home; you see it in the instinc-
tive attraction he felt for a great man.
But that would have all died out if it had
had nothing to feed on; and we may well
believe, as he certainly believed himself,
that he owed a great deal of what was
best in him to his friendship with Samuel
Johnson.　And good in him there certainly
was.　He has never, even by Carlyle, had

full justice done to him. Protests enough have been entered against Macaulay's ridiculous caricature, but for all that its influence seems to linger even in those who make them. Mr. Leslie Stephen has pointed out the unfairness with which Mrs. Thrale has been treated; but he is not nearly severe enough on the detractors of Boswell. And yet we owe Boswell so much that in his case, if in any, a little blindness to such faults as there are would be excusable, and a generous indignation against all who try to see more than there are would be not merely just, but natural.

After all, what were Boswell's faults? A vanity, the most inordinate and the most *naïve*, and a tendency to drink more than was good for him, which, unhappily, lasted all his life. But vanity is of all faults that for which a man pays most heavily and most immediately; and poor Boswell has surely paid for his. And as for the other unfortunate weakness, we must judge him by the habit of his day. No doubt it is contemptible, after all excuses have been made, but it has not deprived Pitt of our gratitude, and some of us will say that it shall not deprive Boswell.

To count up a man's faults is not nearly such a safe way of getting at the truth

about him as to ask what good men who
knew him thought about him.   There are
not many men who can stand that test
better than Boswell ; for where can better
sponsors be found than Burke and Reynolds and Johnson, each of whom honoured
him with a friendship broken only by
death ?   Burke, too, bore striking testimony to his good nature.   Reynolds
cared enough for him to remember him
in his will, and of Johnson's great affection for him we have a hundred proofs.
Nor have there been many people who
have made character an element of friendship as much as Johnson did.   No
worthless man would have found it tolerable or possible to be much with him.
He could make plenty of allowance for
human weakness, but no man gained his
friendship, unless the main current of his
nature, however feeble and however often
diverted, was at least trying to move in
the right direction.   This was the man
who took so rapidly to Boswell, that
when he had only known him ten weeks,
he went with him down to Harwich
to see him set sail for Holland ; who
declared that the more he was seen
the more he would be liked ; who was
himself " glad, very glad " to see him,

and wrote to him again and again in such a strain as—

"My dear Boswell, do not neglect to write to me ; for your kindness is one of the pleasures of my life." "Never, my dear Sir, do you take it into your head to think that I do not love you ; you may settle yourself in full confidence both of my love and my esteem ; I love you as a kind man, I value you as a worthy man, and hope in time to reverence you as a man of exemplary piety. I hold you, as Hamlet has it, 'in my heart of hearts.'"

The world has been mistaken in Johnson if the man to whom he wrote in this way was either fool or scamp.

Nor is Boswell's character dependent on the testimony of a few friends. Is it likely that the gentlemen of Ayrshire would have appointed any but a man of sense and integrity as their "*Præses*" or chairman? They appointed Boswell. Is it likely that the Royal Academy, who filled their honorary offices with such men as Johnson, Goldsmith, and Gibbon, would have invited a fool to be their Secretary for Foreign Correspondence? They invited Boswell. These two facts, even if they stood alone, would be enough to refute Macaulay's disgraceful libel.

That has long been felt to be one of the productions which most injure his fame, and there is no occasion here to slay the slain ; but one thing I may take space to remark, because it has not received the attention it deserves.   Where the whole is absurd, there is, perhaps, no statement more outrageous than that which asserts that in all Boswell's books there is " not a single remark of his own which is not either commonplace or absurd."   I will not labour the point by illustrations : the answer is in every man's knowledge.   I confidently ask of every reader of the great " Life " whether Boswell has not, again and again, not once, but fifty times, given admirably, in a manner far above commonplace, the real sense and truth of some subject which Johnson, " talking for victory," had brought into hopeless topsey-turveydom ?

The fact is that, to arrive at a true idea of Boswell, no great deduction need be made from the impression produced by the letters which passed between him and Johnson.   No doubt he wished Johnson to think as well of him as possible ; but to hide his weaknesses was the last achievement possible to Boswell.   The correspondence is as open and sincere as possible, and does them both credit. Boswell is always ready to confess and receive counsel. Johnson's affection never wavers, his advice and help never fail. Hear him when he had known his future biographer only a few months, writing to direct his studies at Leyden. He gives, incidentally, a curious sketch of the young Boswell.

"You know a gentleman, who, when first he set his foot in the gay world, as he prepared himself to whirl in the vortex of pleasure, imagined a total indifference and universal negligence to be the most agreeable concomitants of youth, and the strongest indication of an airy temper and a quick apprehension. Vacant to every object, and sensible of every impulse, he thought that all appearance of diligence would deduct something from the reputation of genius; and hoped that he should appear to attain, amidst all the ease of carelessness, and all the tumult of diversion, that knowledge and those accomplishments which mortals of the common fabrick obtain only by mute abstraction and solitary drudgery. He tried this scheme of life awhile, was made weary of it by his sense and his virtue; he then wished to return to his studies; and finding long habits of idleness and pleasure harder to be cured than he expected, still willing to retain his claim to some extraordinary prerogatives, resolved the common consequences of irregularity into an unalterable decree of destiny, and concluded that Nature had originally formed him incapable of rational employment.

"Let all such fancies, illusive and destructive, be banished henceforward from your thoughts for ever. Resolve, and keep your resolution; choose, and pursue your choice. If you spend this day in study, you will find yourself still more able to study to-morrow : not that you are to expect that you shall at once obtain a complete victory. Depravity is not very easily overcome. . . . Let me have a long letter from you as soon as you can. I hope you continue your journal, and enrich it with many observations upon the country in which you reside. It will be a favour if you can get me any works in the Frisick language, and can enquire how the poor are maintained in the Seven Provinces."

The last touch sounds very modern : but Johnson always declared that the true criterion of a nation's civilization was the state of its poor. The rest is not the letter he would have written to a young man of no promise. He evidently believed in the " sense and virtue " then, as he still did sixteen years later, when he introduced Boswell to Wesley—

" because I think it very much to be wished that worthy and religious men should be acquainted with each other."

It is still as true as it was when the Greek philosopher first said it that real friendship is only possible between good men ; and when Johnson wrote that Boswell's kindness was one of the pleasures of his life, was it more than a pardonable exaggeration for Boswell, assuring him in reply of his affection and reverence, to add :

" I do not believe that a more perfect attachment ever existed in the history of mankind. And it is a noble attachment; for the attractions are Genius, Learning, and Piety " ?

Johnson was indeed quite alive to Boswell's weaknesses. We have seen the picture he painted of them in the letter sent to Leyden ; and he is as unwearied in his attempts to steady Boswell's " volatility," as he is outspoken in his contempt of his fanciful melancholy. Boswell was, in truth, a little proud of both ; so that it was necessary to speak plainly. No one will deny that gift to Johnson ; and he used it freely for Boswell's benefit.

" Read Cheyne's *English Malady ;* but do not let him teach you a foolish notion that melancholy is a proof of acuteness. . . . I am, I confess, very angry that you manage yourself so ill." " When any fit of anxiety, or gloominess, or perversion of mind, lays hold upon you, make it a rule not to publish it by complaints, but exert your whole care to hide it ; by endeavouring to hide it, you will drive it away. Be always busy." " The great direction which Burton has left to men disordered like you, is this, *Be not solitary ; be not idle :* which I would thus modify ; If you are idle, be not solitary ; if you are solitary, be not idle." " Get rid of all intellectual excesses, and neither exalt your pleasures nor aggravate your vexations, beyond their real and natural state. . . . Please yourself with your wife and children, and studies and practice." " You are always complaining of melancholy, and I conclude from those complaints that you are fond of it.   No man talks of that which he is desirous to conceal, and every man desires to conceal that of which he is ashamed.   Do not pretend to deny it: *manifestum habemus furem:* make it an invariable and obligatory law to yourself, never to mention your own mental diseases: if you are never to speak of them you will think on them but little, and if you think little of them, they will molest you rarely."   "Dear Sir, I hoped you had got rid of all this hypocrisy of misery.   What have you to do with Liberty and Necessity ?   Or what more than to hold your tongue about it?"

The mental or physical *malade imaginaire* is indeed of all people the most difficult to bear with : and that in his own interest, for to bear with him is simply to aggravate his disease: but in this case Johnson may have felt himself to be unduly severe, for his real kindliness of feeling comes in a few lines lower to soothe the wound :

"Come to me, my dear Bozzy, and let us be as happy as we can."

One may note that his advice is absolutely disinterested ; he is thinking of Boswell's good, and that alone.   Neither Lord Auchinleck, for instance, nor Mrs. Boswell, liked Johnson ; yet there are no duties which he impresses on Boswell more earnestly and repeatedly than those he owed to his father and his wife.

"I had great pleasure in hearing that you are at last on good terms with your father.   Cultivate his kindness by all honest and manly means." "You ought to think it no small inducement to diligence and perseverance, that they will please your father." "Make your father as happy as you can."

So, again, in the midst of exhortations to economy:

"One expense, however, I would not have you to spare: let nothing be omitted that can preserve Mrs. Boswell, though it should be necessary to transplant her for a time into a softer climate. She is the prop and stay of your life."

Economy is, one may remark, a subject on which he speaks very strongly, at least to Boswell. He was afraid that Boswell would rush into extravagances on succeeding his father, and is very anxious to prevent anything of the kind.

"Begin your new course of life with the least show and the least expense possible; you may at pleasure increase both, but you cannot easily diminish them. Do not think your estate your own, while any man can call upon you for money which you cannot pay." "Resolve not to be poor; whatever you have, spend less. Poverty is a great enemy to human happiness; it certainly destroys liberty, and it makes some virtues impracticable, and others extremely difficult." "Of riches it is not necessary to write the praise."

No doubt the opposition between such maxims as these, meant as Johnson meant them, and certain sayings in the Gospels, is only verbal; but it is strange that so self-consciously strict a Christian as Johnson does not appear aware of it at all.

But no isolated passages will give us so complete a picture both of Johnson and Boswell, their characters and their friendship, as a complete letter like this which follows. It was written in answer to one from Boswell,

"requesting his counsel whether I should, this spring, come to London."

There were, on the one hand, pecuniary embarrassments and his wife's state of health ; on the other

" the pleasure and improvement which my annual visit to the metropolis always afforded," and a " peculiar satisfaction which I experienced in celebrating the festival of Easter in St. Paul's Cathedral."

This is what Johnson wrote. He never wrote a more characteristic letter :

" DEAR SIR,—I am ashamed to think that since I received your letter I have passed so many days without answering it.

" I think there is no great difficulty in resolving your doubts. The reasons for which you are in-clined to visit London are, I think, not of sufficient strength to answer the objections. That you should delight to come once a year to the fountain of intelligence and pleasure, is very natural ; but both information and pleasure must be regulated by propriety. Pleasure, which cannot be obtained but by unseasonable or unsuitable expense, must always end in pain; and pleasure, which must be enjoyed at the expense of another's pain, can never be such as a worthy mind can fully delight in.

"What improvement you might gain by coming to London, you may easily supply, or easily compensate, by enjoining yourself some particular study at home, or opening some new avenue to information. Edinburgh is not yet exhausted; and I am sure you will find no pleasure here which can deserve either that you should anticipate any part of your future fortune, or that you should condemn yourself and your lady to penurious frugality for the rest of the year.

"I need not tell you what regard you owe to Mrs. Boswell's entreaties; or how much you ought to study the happiness of her who studies yours with so much diligence, and of whose kindness you enjoy such good effects. Life cannot subsist in society but by reciprocal concessions. She permitted you to ramble last year, you must permit her now to keep you at home.

"Your last reason is so serious that I am unwilling to oppose it. Yet you must remember, that your image of worshipping once a year in a certain place, in imitation of the Jews, is but a comparison; and *simile non est idem :* if the annual resort to Jerusalem was a duty to the Jews, it was a duty because it was commanded; and you have no such command, therefore no such duty. It may be dangerous to receive too readily, and indulge too fondly, opinions, from which, perhaps, no pious mind is wholly disengaged, of local sanctity and local devotion. You know what strange effects they have produced over a great part of the Christian world. I am now writing, and you, when you read this, are reading, under the Eye of Omnipresence.

"To what degree fancy is to be admitted into religious offices it would require much deliberation to determine. I am far from intending totally to exclude it. Fancy is a faculty bestowed by our Creator, and it is reasonable that all His gifts should be used to His glory, that all our faculties should co-operate in His worship; but they are to co-operate according to the will of Him that gave them, according to the order which His wisdom has established. As ceremonies prudential or convenient are less obligatory than positive ordinances, as bodily worship is only the token to others or ourselves of mental adoration, so Fancy is always to act in subordination to Reason. We may take Fancy for a companion, but must follow Reason as our guide. We may allow Fancy to suggest certain ideas in certain places; but Reason must always be heard, when she tells us, that those ideas and those places have no natural or necessary relation. When we enter a church we habitually recall to mind the duty of adoration, but we must not omit adoration for want of a temple; because we know, and ought to remember, that the Universal Lord is everywhere present; and that, therefore, to come to Iona, or to Jerusalem, though it may be useful, cannot be necessary.

"Thus I have answered your letter, and have not answered it negligently. I love you too well to be careless when you are serious."

"Not negligently!" There would be more letters written for advice, and to more purpose, if the answers could oftener come back like this, luminous, eloquent, masterly; rich, one may say, in the wisdom, both of Reason and of

Religion. And note that it is a real answer; and not, as so often happens, a dissertation on some subject interesting to the writer, but on which no opinion has been asked. The points are throughout Boswell's points, not Johnson's; he has not deserted them for a moment, though he has treated them in a manner far above the narrowness of mere personal or occasional application. The business of literature and art is sometimes said to be to see the universal in the particular. It is not performed every day as this letter performs it.

And what a picture of Johnson himself! The man of plain common sense is in it, and so is the affectionate friend; but the ethical philosopher, the Christian moralist, above all the saint, the man of personal religion, are still more conspicuous. The whole serious side of him is there, in fact; only the lighter side is not to be found in it. It required, indeed, a more potent spell than Boswell or any of Boswell's sex possessed to induce Johnson to put that into his letters.

The letters to Mrs. Thrale are certainly the best Johnson ever wrote. They do not indeed give us the deeper side of the man as those he wrote to Boswell do; for Mrs. Thrale had nothing of Boswell's

sincere religious feeling, and Johnson could
not write what she would not have understood.   He often writes very seriously to
her, of course, as he did to every one, but
not with the fulness which he could use
to Boswell in all assurance of sympathy
and response.   The interest of the Thrale
series lies in their comparative wealth of
detail, in their greater lightness of heart
and of touch, in more frequent humour, in
a nearer approach, that is, to the ideal
of what a letter should be.   They are
also remarkable for their literary allusions,
and quotations, as well as for a peculiar
gallantry, which Johnson affected towards
Mrs. Thrale. A curious chapter might
be written on the history of his relations with the other sex.   There was his
elderly wife, his fervent adoration of whom
has its touching and beautiful side in the
prayers he continued to offer for her, " so
far as is lawful," throughout his life, as
well as its humorous one in his styling
her " my charming love " when she was
fifty-one, and perhaps in their daily life, if
one may believe the story of her saying
to him at dinner, " Nay, hold, Mr. Johnson,
and do not make a farce of thanking God
for a dinner which in a few minutes you
will protest not eatable."   Then there was

her daughter, who, as he told Mrs. Thrale, had " many excellencies very noble and resplendent, though a little discoloured by hoary virginity." Those remarkable ladies, Mrs. Williams and Mrs. Desmoulins, whom his charity maintained at Bolt Court, are sufficiently well known. They had their virtues, no doubt, but what we most think of in connection with them is their incessant squabbling. " Williams hates everybody. Levett hates Desmoulins, and does not love Williams. Desmoulins hates them both. Poll loves none of them." Of " Poll " we also possess the remarkable trait that when talked to " tightly and closely " nothing could be made of her : " she was wiggle-waggle, and I could never persuade her to be categorical." Then there are all the ladies with whom his relations, though only occasional, are often curious, from the great Mrs. Montagu, whose affectation of equality he quelled by proposing that her footman should dine with them, and who perhaps has the honour of being the only person to whom he was ever insincere, to the "very decent girl in a printed linen," who made tea for him in Glenmorrison, and "engaged" him so much that he made her a present of Cocker's Arithmetic.

There is no record of her gratitude. But the woman whose name far more than any other will always be connected with his is, of course, Mrs. Thrale, whose house was his home, and to whom he wrote more than three hundred letters. They are not perfect. There are too many, as was his wont, occupied only with morals, and far too many occupied only with medicine. In morals he was a master, and though the taste of to-day is easily sated with such food, we must remember that it was not so in his day; and, besides, his moralising is sound even for us by being not only often powerful, but always of an almost unique sincerity. In medicine, on the other hand, he was only a dabbler; and, however much pleasure he may have found in dilating with the anxious particularity of a *dilettante* on the maladies of himself and his friends and their appropriate remedies, we may be excused for not caring to follow him. But even if morals and medicine are both put aside, there is plenty of good stuff left in the letters. Above all, there is plenty of pleasant evidence of the gratitude and affection he felt towards his " Master " and " Mistress."

" Such tattle as filled your last sweet letter."
" I do love to hear from you. Such pretty, kind

letters as you send. But it gives me great delight to find that my master misses me." "I cannot but think on your kindness and my master's. Life has, upon the whole, fallen short, very short, of my early expectation ; but the acquisition of such a friendship, at an age when new friendships are seldom acquired, is something better than the general course of things gives man a right to expect. I think on it with great delight; I am not very apt to be delighted." "And so, because you hear that Mrs. Desmoulins has written, you hold it not necessary to write; as if she could write like you, or I were equally content with hearing from her. Call you this, backing your friends ? She did write, and I remember nothing in her letter but that she was discontented that I wrote only Madam to her, and Dear Madam to Mrs. Williams. Without any great dearness in the comparison, Williams is, I think, the dearer of the two. . . . But at Streatham there are dears and dears, who, before this letter reaches them, will be at Brighthelmstone. Wherever they be, may they have no uneasiness but for want of me."

Passages of this kind abound in the letters. He could never hear enough about them and their children and their affairs.

"Let me have kind letters full of yourself, of your own hopes, and your own fears, and your own thoughts, and then go where you will."

He is always looking at the barley crop and inquiring after probabilities of prices for the sake of Mr. Thrale and the brewery.

He takes a great interest in a regatta if his mistress is to be there.

"I am glad that you are to be at the regatta. You know how little I love to have you left out of any shining part of life. . . . It is easy to talk of sitting at home contented, when others are seeing or making shows. But not to have been where it is supposed, and seldom supposed falsely, that all would go if they could . . . is, after all, a state of temporary inferiority, in which the mind is rather hardened by stubbornness, than supported by fortitude. If the world be worth winning, let us enjoy it; if it is to be despised, let us despise it by conviction."

And two days later:

"So now you have been at the regatta, for I hope you got tickets somewhere, else you wanted me, and I shall not be sorry, because you fancy you can do so well without me; but however I hope you got tickets, and were dressed fine and fanciful, and made a fine part of the fine show, and heard musick, and said good things, and staid on the water four hours after midnight, and came well home, and slept, and dreamed of the regatta, and waked, and found yourself in bed, and thought now it is all over, only I must write about it to Lichfield."

All the doings of the family interest him. He indulges in humorous rejoicings over Mrs. Thrale's abandonment of her wig: "Everybody was an enemy to that wig. We will burn it and get drunk; for what is joy without drink"; and in more serious ones over Mr. Thrale's planting : "I take great delight in your fifteen thousand trees." One remembers Edward FitzGerald's saying, " all magnanimous men love trees." He takes the greatest interest in the growing profits of the brewery, and will find sympathy for the " gravelling and walling and digging," and all the other ways Mr. Thrale had of getting rid of his money—except, indeed, the foolish craze for "out-brewing Whitbread." The rest he likes to hear about, though, for his own part, if he had the money he would prefer to "go to Cairo and down the Red Sea to Bengal, and take a ramble in India." Nothing shows his affection and intimacy more than the frank way in which he asks for what he wants. " Could you not send me something out of your garden ? I wish I had a great bunch of asparagus." " Mrs. Williams has been very ill, and it would do her good if you would send a message of enquiry, and a few strawberries or currants." " Some old gentlewomen at the next door are in very great distress. . . . Persuade my master to let me give them something for him." " The harvest is abundant, and the weather *à la merveille*. . . . Barley, malt, beer, and money. There is the series of ideas. The deep logicians call

it a *sorites.* I hope my master will no
longer endure the reproach of not keeping
me a horse." The letters abound, too,
with affectionate allusions to the children.
In one there is a curious account of his
going to see two of them, because he
thinks their mother may be anxious.

"That you may have no superfluous uneasiness,
I went this afternoon to visit the two babies at
Kensington, and found them indeed a little spotted
with their disorder, but as brisk and gay as health
and youth can make them. I took a paper of
sweetmeats, and spread them on the table. They
took great delight to shew their governess the
various animals that were made of sugar ; and
when they had eaten as much as was fit, the rest
were laid up for to-morrow."

But I must make an end of extracts to
find space for at least one complete letter.
It will show how surprisingly the author
of Rasselas could throw off his full-
bottomed wig when he pleased. Here is
one from Lichfield comparatively early in
their acquaintance :

"I set out on Thursday morning, and found my
companion, to whom I was very much a stranger,
more agreeable than I expected. We went cheer-
fully forward and passed the night at Coventry.
We came in late, and went out early ; and therefore
I did not send for my cousin Tom ; but I design
to make him some amends for the omission.

"Next day we came early to Lucy, who was, I

believe, glad to see us. She had saved her best gooseberries upon the tree for me; and, as Steele says, *I was neither too proud nor too wise* to gather them. I have rambled a very little *inter fontes et flumina nota*, but I am not yet well. They have cut down the trees in George Lane. Evelyn, in his book of Forest Trees, tells us of wicked men that cut down trees and never prospered afterwards; yet nothing has deterred these audacious aldermen from violating the Hamadryads of George Lane. As an impartial traveller I must however tell, that in Stow Street, where I left a draw-well, I have found a pump; but the lading-well in this ill-fated George Lane lies shamefully neglected.

"I am going to-day or to-morrow to Ashbourne; but I am at a loss how I shall get back in time to London. Here are only chance coaches, so that there is no certainty of a place. If I do not come, let it not hinder your journey. I can be but a few days behind you; and I will follow in the Brighthelmstone coach. But I hope to come.

"I took care to tell Miss Porter that I have got another Lucy. I hope she is well. Tell Mrs. Salisbury that I beg her stay at Streatham for little Lucy's sake."

This is one from Ashbourne in 1777:

"DEAR MADAM,—I think I have already told you that Bos. is gone. The day before he went we met the Duke and Duchess of Argyle in the street, and went to speak to them while they changed horses; and in the afternoon Mrs. Langton and Juliet stopped in their way to London, and sent for me; I went to them, and sent for Boswell, whom Mrs. Langton had never seen.

"And so, here is this post without a letter. 'I am old, I am old,' says Sir John Falstaff. 'Take heed, my dear, youth flies apace.' You will be wanting a letter some time. I wish I were with you, but I cannot come yet.

> " ' Nives et frigora Rheni
> Me sine sola vides: Ah, ne te frigora laedant!
> Ah, tibi ne teneras glacies secet aspera plantas!'

"I wish you well; B—— and all; and shall be glad to know your adventures. Do not, however, think wholly to escape me; you will, I hope, see me at Brighthelmstone. Dare you answer me as Brutus answered his evil genius?

"I know not when I shall write again, now you are going to the world's end. *Extra anni solisque vias*, where the post will be a long time in reaching you. I shall, notwithstanding all distance, continue to think on you, and to please myself with the hope of being once again, Madam,

"Your most humble servant,

"Sam: Johnson."

Every one will admit that this is a delightful letter, with just the lightness of touch one loves in a letter and misses, as a rule, in Johnson. Its quotations from Shakespeare and Virgil are especially characteristic of the letters to his "mistress." There are ten in what he wrote to her for one in the other letters. No doubt it was a form of flattery to a clever woman. It is curious to note the authors he quotes: the frequent misquotations show that he relied entirely on his memory. I have been at the pains to count the authors cited. Virgil and Horace appear fourteen times each, Shakspeare thirteen times, Ovid eight, Dryden seven, Pope six, Milton five, Juvenal and Swift four, Cowley three times, Addison, Lee, Rowe, and the Bible twice, Aristotle, Terence, Lucretius, Cicero, Martial, Tacitus, Hadrian, Sulpicius Severus, Erasmus, Molière, La Rochefoucauld, La Bruyère, Madame de Maintenon, Trissino, Burton, Sidney, Walsh, Richardson, Locke, Thompson, Congreve, Evelyn, Young, and Percy once each. Probably a few have been over-looked ; meanwhile it is a long list already, and one is glad that Virgil and Horace, with Shakespeare, are at the head of it. The most curious omission is perhaps that of Collins, who had been his friend. One is not so surprised at the absence of Gray, whom he notoriously disliked ; and Catullus, Chaucer, and Spenser, the only quite first-class names in Latin and English poetry not quoted in the letters, were little known in the eighteenth century. Not that that would by any means make it certain that he would not have read them. In fact, he is pretty sure to have done so. It was a very large literary country which he hunted over. We have seen Trissino and Sulpicius Severus; and one remembers the Harwich journey on which he read *Pomponius Mela de situ Orbis*, when he was not engaged in defending the Inquisition, or expounding the laws of Holland to an unfortunate Dutchman who had tried to curry favour with him by preferring those of England.

His letters give us fewer glimpses of his literary friends and contemporaries than we could wish. There are several references to Collins, whose terrible malady was the one which Johnson most dreaded for himself.

"Poor, dear Collins! Let me know whether you think it would give him pleasure if I should write to him. I have often been near his state, and therefore have it in great commiseration."

And, elsewhere : " that man is no common loss." He tells Boswell in July, 1774,. that there is little, except debts, to add to what the papers had told of " poor dear Dr. Goldsmith," who had died in April. Reynolds is once mentioned as having " taken too much to strong liquor"; but it must be remembered that Johnson was a water-drinker. Johnson tells Boswell that Beattie is " so caressed, and invited, and treated, and liked, and flattered, by the great that I can see nothing of him. I am in great hope that he will be well provided for, and then we will live upon him at the Marischal College, without pity or modesty." Beauclerk's death is just mentioned : " Poor dear Beauclerk—*nec ut soles dabis joca.*" It is a meagre list. The fact is, Johnson's space is filled with his correspondents and himself, and the abundant reflections which their doings and sufferings suggest to a mind like his. Of himself the picture is essentially the same as that Boswell drew, though it necessarily wants the vivacity of the talker in the " Life." Still even in the letters we find that he can not only indulge in chaff with Mrs. Thrale, but also in other indications of constitutional sprightliness triumphing over the gravity, corporal as well as moral, of a philosopher. When only a year or two short of seventy he runs a race with Baretti in the rain at Paris and beats him. At fifty he proposed to a Regius Professor, " eminent for learning and worth," and " of an ancient and respectable family," to climb over a wall for the fun of it. The proposal, it should be added, was very properly refused. Indeed, learned as he was, he was no mere bookworm. He was, it has been well pointed out, the last of the old scholars, as opposed to the modern men of letters. The distinction between the two may perhaps be said to consist in the fact that the business of the one was to know and by no means necessarily to write, while the business of the other is to write and by no means necessarily to know. But, scholar or man of letters, the essential thing in his eyes was that a man should take a liberal view of life, should approach it from the intellectual and moral side. He had a scholar's contempt for " the boobies of Birmingham "; and wanted something more than business to fill his mind.

" On Monday," he writes once, " we hope to see Birmingham, the seat of the mechanick arts ; and know not whether our next stage will be Oxford, the mansion of the liberal arts; or London, the residence of all the arts together. The chymists call the world *Academia Paracelsi :* my ambition is to be his fellow-student—to see the works of nature and hear the lectures of truth. To London, there-fore—London may perhaps fill me ; and I hope to fill my part of London."

He calmed Mrs. Thrale's fears about the brewery, too, with a serene disbelief in the mysteries of business, which scholars cannot always bring to support their feeling of superiority : " Trade could not be managed by those who manage it, if it had much difficulty."

But scholar and book-lover as he was, he never for a moment ceases to be a very human figure. In literature itself, he insisted on the value of the graceful and "elegant" side, declaring that a "mere antiquarian is a rugged being." No mere recluse could have written, as he did, in language which recalls FitzGerald in Charlotte Street:

"I hope to see standing corn in some part of the earth this Summer, but I shall hardly smell hay, or suck clover flowers."

He was human enough to love not merely his friends, but his dinner. He alternated, as is well known, between voracity and abstinence, the usual case of people who, in his phrase, "mind their bellies" too fondly. He tells Mrs. Thrale that he cannot help it, for his "genius" is always in extremes.

"Last week I saw flesh but twice, and, I think, fish once; the rest was pease. You are afraid, you say, lest I extenuate myself too fast, and are an enemy to violence; but did you never hear nor read, dear Madam, that every man has his *genius*, and that the great rule by which all excellence is attained, is to follow *genius*; and have you not observed in all our conversations that my *genius* is always in extremes; that I am very noisy or very silent; very gloomy or very merry; very sour or very kind? And would you have me cross my *genius*, when it leads me sometimes to voracity and sometimes to abstinence ? "

There are some men who seem to walk through life always erect and radiant, aiming at a definite goal, reaching it at the predetermined moment, doing admirable work, satisfying themselves and filling others with admiration. Gibbon, for instance, was just such a man. Johnson was the very reverse. He did a great deal, but he took no pleasure in his achievements. All his works but one were produced under the stimulus of want ; and all alike were, as it were, dragged out of him against his will, and finished long after they were due. The value and attraction of the other type of character is real and obvious ; but in a moral balance who can tell which is to weigh heavier, the unfailing self-control, the uninterrupted triumph, of Gibbon, or the broken resolutions, so bitterly felt, of Johnson ?   When he was at work he wished only to be at liberty ; and yet

" What would I do if I was at liberty ?   Would I go to Mrs. Aston and Mrs. Porter, and see the old places, and sigh to find that my old friends are gone ?   Would I recall plans of life which I never brought into practice, and hopes of excellence which I once presumed and never have attained ?

Would I compare what I now am with what I once expected to have been? Is it reasonable to wish for suggestions of shame and opportunities of sorrow?"

So, again, when he knew he was dying, he wrote:

"You know I never thought confidence with respect to futurity any part of the character of a brave, a wise, or a good man. Bravery has no place where it can avail nothing; wisdom impresses strongly the consciousness of those faults, of which it is itself perhaps an aggravation; and goodness, always wishing to be better, and imputing every deficience to criminal negligence, and every fault to voluntary corruption, never dares to suppose the condition of forgiveness fulfilled, nor what is wanting in the crime supplied by penitence.

"This is the state of the best, but what must be the condition of him whose heart will not suffer him to rank himself among the best, or among the good?"

To turn from this to the "Memoirs of my Life and Writings" is simply to enter another world. Gibbon's cheerful optimism would have seen nothing in what Johnson writes but the absurd self-tortures of a weak "enthusiasm." And the "Decline and Fall" is there to justify its author's theory of life. Utilitarianism, looking wholly at results, would have no difficulty in judging between him and Johnson. But Christianity, which looks behind them, at aspirations unrealized, at tasks begun though never completed, may perhaps arrive at a different verdict. In any case, it is quite possible to feel not only the sincerest gratitude to Gibbon for his great legacy, but also the heartiest liking for his cheerful good sense and good temper, and yet to recognise that there was something in Johnson which was quite out of his reach. Kind he may be, possessed of real sympathy, at times even self-denying; but in the deepest things of life, the hopes and fears and doubts in which humanity finds its highest voice, he is a trifler or a child. It was just in these things that Johnson's real life lay; Johnson, who could not repeat the " Dies Iræ " without bursting into tears, in whose eyes that man was fitter to be called an animal than a human being who could pass through life without giving the most solemn and constant thought to the supreme problems of his origin and his destiny.

GIBBON.[1]

GIBBON is not only our greatest historian; he is also, if we put poets aside, one of our half-dozen greatest men of letters. His unique position as a historian is amply proved by the fact that there is no other history, in a modern language, treating of a period not the author's own, which is anything like so widely and frequently read, a hundred years after publication, as his is still to-day. But he owes at least half his readers to other than historical merits. Mere admiration for the courage which conceived a vast undertaking, for the learning which justified it, or for the masterly and luminous handling which alone could give shape to material so immense, would not by itself have caused the Decline and Fall to survive its author longer than anything

[1] First printed in the " Fortnightly Review," March, 1897, under the title " The Man Gibbon." The only complete edition of Gibbon's Letters is the " Private Letters of Edward Gibbon," with an Introduction by the Earl of Sheffield, edited by Rowland E. Prothero, in two volumes, Murray, 1896.

in English prose, of at all equal bulk
and seriousness.   It is even possible that
nothing equally old has so many readers
to-day, if we except Bacon's " Essays,"
" The Pilgrim's Progress," " Robinson
Crusoe," Goldsmith's " Vicar," and Boswell's "Johnson"; and if this is so, it is to
the man of letters and not to the historian
that it is due.   It is not so much by what he
tells us as by his incomparable way of telling
it that he attracts us.   Like every great
artist he has given us himself as well as his
subject, and if we return again and again
to the Decline and Fall, it is less for the
sake of Byzantine Emperors and Gothic
invaders than for that of Gibbon himself.
We feel the presence, behind every page,
almost behind every sentence, of a great
and original personality.

The publication of the original manuscripts of the famous Memoirs, and of a
large number of new Letters, has lately
placed us for the first time in a position
to know all that there is to be known
about Gibbon.   It cannot be said that it
seriously affects our judgment of him.   The
new volumes are delightful reading, but
we hardly know him any better when we
have finished them than we did before we
began : we have only seen more of him.

But Edward Gibbon is one of those people of whom we cannot see too much, and we are heartily grateful to Lord Sheffield, Mr. Murray, and Mr. Prothero, for the new opportunities they have given us.

We now possess the complete picture of him which is, of course, to be looked for partly in the Memoirs and partly in the Letters. It had long been known that the Memoirs as hitherto published were an arrangement put together by Lord Sheffield or his daughter from several sketches left by Gibbon. These have now been printed for the first time. But the bulk, and the best, of what Gibbon wrote, has already appeared in his editor's brilliant compilation. The new matter affords a good many characteristic touches, hitherto suppressed by editorial prudence or prudery, and the whole opens out an interesting problem to the curious: but that interest centres round the personality of the editor rather than that of the author, and the large public who care more for Gibbon than for the Holroyds, decidedly prefer the short to the long, and dislike repetition, will prefer the single old autobiography to the seven new. To talk of that incomparable production would be, it may be hoped, to talk of

what everyone knows more than very well
—everyone at least who cares at all for
literature—for the "Memoirs of my Life
and Writings" are, and deserve to be,
almost the Bible of all sorts and conditions
of students.   But the case is different with
the letters.   Here the new matter is much
more extensive than the old, and even the
old was never well known as the Memoirs
were.   It is true that Lord Sheffield
printed the best of the letters, and that
the new ones do not materially alter our
conception of Gibbon.   But it is also true
that Lord Sheffield subjected the letters
which he published to a very rude and
merciless pruning; that they are consequently full of irritating blanks and
asterisks; and that they are very awk-
wardly arranged in two separate batches.
There can, therefore, be no doubt that,
if the public keeps to the old Memoirs,
it will prefer the new letters.   In Mr.
Prothero's two volumes we have most of
the old letters, printed for the first time
in full as Gibbon wrote them, and about
four hundred new ones.   They are of every
kind, but the largest divisions of them are
Gibbon's business letters to his father,
his unbroken correspondence with his
stepmother after she settled at Bath, the

business portions of his letters to Lord Sheffield, which had been hitherto omitted, and Lord Sheffield's replies. The whole forms a most interesting and delightful collection; but as gratitude is never perfect in this world, there are one or two reserves to make. It is, perhaps, hardly worth mentioning that at least one or two letters, and some parts of letters, which were already known, have not been marked with the asterisks which are said to distinguish what has been already published from what has not. The index, too, might well have been a little fuller. Under the heading, for instance, of "Hon. Maria Holroyd," it only refers us to Gibbon's letters to her and hers to him, not to the letters in which Gibbon and her father speak of her ability. A more important point is that the two volumes, while reprinting many, do not reprint all the old letters, and consequently are not complete. None of the early letters to foreign scholars are reprinted. They may, however, be considered rather treatises than letters. But the letters to and from Robertson, Watson, Adam Smith, and others of a similar kind, given in the old editions, might surely be retained with advantage in spite of their formality. Again, one of the letters to Cadell, the bookseller, is given, but not the one which contains the well-known remarks about Boswell and Johnson: "Boswell's book will be curious, or at least whimsical; his hero, who can so long detain the public curiosity, must be no common animal." And there are other instances. No doubt the new edition does not pretend to be complete, but prints I suppose only what has been found at Sheffield Place. But when a collection is so nearly complete as this is, would it not be just as well to make it absolutely so? Let us hope that this will be done when a second edition appears, and that a good table of contents, or at least a list of the letters, such as we have in the original collection, will be added. It would be impossible to improve the notes Mr. Prothero has given us. They always appear when they are wanted, and what is equally important, never when they are not wanted. They are all full, but not too full, of interest and information. Not least among their merits is that of preserving a number of good stories. We have Burke on the Board of Trade, Fox on Gibbon, Gibbon on Pitt, and Lord North on himself. One of the best is that of the Duke of Gloucester on the Decline and Fall. When his second volume appeared, Gibbon presented it to the Duke, who " received the author with much good nature and affability," saying to him, as he laid the quarto on the table, " Another d—mn'd thick, square book! Always scribble, scribble, scribble! eh! Mr. Gibbon ? "

Gibbon's mind and the style which is the reflection of it are more at home in the atmosphere of a work which must and should be deliberate, formal and, in the best sense, artificial, than in the lighter, more familiar and occasional, epistolary world. Not that art has not a great deal to do with the making of a good letter, but it is an art, as one cannot too often repeat, whose principal characteristics are ease, grace, delicacy, variety, lightness of touch, and these are not the things we look for from Gibbon. But, if his style is not everything the critical heart might desire, its merits must not be forgotten. It is formal, and even pompous, no doubt. But there are two classes of pompous writers. The more common is that which prefers high-sounding phrases, because they are the best protection of those who have nothing to say. The other is that

which, having something, and something
of weight and importance to say, is determined to give it all the advantages of a
stately and splendid presentation ; and so
runs the risk, in its dread of vulgarity, of
being betrayed into the opposite extreme.
It was to this class that Gibbon belonged.
He set a very high value upon style.
Even when he receives Lord Sheffield's
political publications, we find him more
than once hinting his regret that his
friend is " above the trifling decorations
of style and order."   And for himself we
know that he would take several turns
round his table before he could settle a
period to his satisfaction.   The stately
structure of his sentences remains for ever
in just and immortal association with the
stateliness of his theme : and if the
preference, which had become a habit,
occasionally degenerated into an abuse,
who that loves dignity in a slipshod age
will care to condemn very severely a fault
that came of loving it too well?   Language
that is over-formal is easily forgiven, so
long as there is sense and meaning behind
it ; and few indeed are the authors who
have surpassed Gibbon in his strict
observance of the rule that every sentence
ought to contribute something, great or

small, to the argument or theme of its author. There is besides a special excuse for his elaborate formality as it appears in the letters. It was a habit, no doubt, which he could not easily have broken, but it is clear that he often used it deliberately and consciously for the sake of the humorous effect it produces. When he writes, for instance, to Mrs. Gibbon, on the birth of one of Lord Sheffield's daughters: "yesterday afternoon about half an hour past five a young *Lady* was introduced into the world, and though her sex might be considered an objection, she was received with great politeness"; or when, in telling Lady Sheffield of the numerous merits, liveliness, sincerity, capacity as a nurse, dignity at the head of his table, and economy in its management, which he would be exacting enough to desire in a wife, he remarks: "could I find all these qualities united in a single person, I should dare to make my addresses and should deserve to be refused," he is purposely pompous and is well aware of what he is doing. He intended Mrs. Gibbon and Lady Sheffield to be amused, and no doubt they were; and so are we. So again when his stepmother, as he tells Lord Sheffield, "started two very ingenious objections " to his going to Paris in 1777, he must have smiled as he penned the balanced antitheses of his reply. The objections were; " 1st, that I shall be confined or put to death by the priests, and 2nd that I shall sully my *moral* character by making love to Necker's wife " (the Mdlle. Curchod over whom he had "sighed as a lover" in his youth). Here is part of his reply which Lord Sheffield very naturally suppressed :

"When you have indulged the exquisite sensibility of friendship, you will, I am sure, make a proper use of your excellent understanding, and will soon smile at your own terrors. The constancy and danger of a twenty years' passion is a subject upon which I hardly know how to be serious. I am ignorant what effect that period of time has had upon me, but I do assure you that it has committed great ravages upon the Lady, and that at present she is very far from being an object either of desire or scandal. . . . I have not the least reason to believe that they think of offering me an apartment, but if they do, I shall certainly refuse it, for the sake of my own comfort and freedom ; so that the husband will be easy, the world will be mute, and my *moral* character will still preserve its immaculate purity."

As to the danger from the clergy, he serenely observes : "The wisdom of the Government and the liberal temper of the

Nation have rendered these monsters perfectly inoffensive."

In this way the uniformity of his style brings its own compensation. And, in any case, the interest of a collection of letters lies so largely in the personality of the writer that, when that is as rich and interesting as it is in Gibbon's case, we can afford to put other considerations aside. The charm of self-revelation saves all. There may be an affectation in manner, but there is none in matter. The letters show us the great historian just as he was. They prove, as Lord Sheffield said, "how pleasant, friendly, and amiable Mr. Gibbon was in private life"; but they do much more than that. They are generally very full and outspoken, and the best of them are not far from being as egotistical as a good letter ought to be. Everything goes into them; his books and his friends, his likes and his dislikes, his dread of the approach of the gout, and his desire for the arrival of an overdue cask of Madeira: something is contributed by the morning hours in the study, something by the cards or visits or amusements which occupied his afternoons; and something, too, by epicurean memories or anticipations of pretty dinners or suppers.

His love of books is there, and his hatred of business: the worldliness which he learnt in the " mixed, though polite, company of Boodle's, White's, and Brookes's "; and the learning which introduced him to " The Club " of Johnson and Burke. There, too, is the " subcynical humour " which Mr. Harrison has dared to confess is not to his taste, but which is certainly one of the features in him which the generality of his readers most clearly remember, and with which they would least willingly part. But perhaps the dominant note of all is one which I have not enumerated, that serene and unfailing optimism which surveys the fortune, the friends, the occupations, and the retreat which fate had provided for him, and rejoices with a rare philosophy as much in what had been refused as in what had been given. It finds its most complete expression, no doubt, in some famous passages in the Memoirs like that in which he says, " when I contemplate the common lot of mortality, I must acknowledge that I have drawn a high prize in the lottery of life," and declares his disgust at " the affectation of men of letters who complain that they have renounced a substance for a shadow." But it is also to be found everywhere in the Letters, especially during his later years at Lausanne. When he had made his exodus from the House of Commons, he gave no more thought to the fleshpots of Egypt, but rather rejoiced in his escape from the daily tale of bricks. Hear him congratulate himself on the contrast between his life and Lord Sheffield's:

"Last Tuesday, November 11th, after plaguing and vexing yourself all the morning about some business of your fertile creation, you went to the House of Commons and passed the afternoon, the evening, and perhaps the night, without sleep or food, stifled in a close room by the heated respiration of six hundred politicians, inflamed by party and passion, and tired of the repetition of dull nonsense which, in that illustrious assembly, so far outweighs the proportion of reason and eloquence. On the same day, after a studious morning, a friendly dinner, and a cheerful assembly of both sexes, I retired to rest at eleven o'clock, satisfied with the past day, and certain that the next would afford me the return of the same quiet and rational enjoyments. *Which has the better bargain?*"

That is his invariable tone. "No. 7, Bentinck Street, is the best house in the world." "I am very glad that I was born." "I enjoy health, friends, reputation, and a perpetual fund of domestic amusement; I am not without resources, and my best resource, which shall never

desert me, is in the cheerfulness and
tranquillity of a mind which, in any place
and in any situation, can always secure
its own independent happiness.''

This last was written on the occasion
of his being turned out of the Board of
Trade; but there is nothing forced or
exceptional about it.   He always looks on
the bright side of things, regrets nothing
that he has given up, wants nothing that
he cannot have.   He has a right to laugh
at the hysterical lamentations of men of
letters, for his own attitude is always
perfectly simple and perfectly dignified.
He does not quarrel either with his pub-
lisher or with the public: he makes no
complaint against Ministers who gave him
neither pensions nor ribbons.   We do not
find him pointing indignant comparisons
between the earnings of a man of genius
and those of a great merchant, or even a
Cabinet Minister: he is perfectly aware
that merchants and statesmen live disagreeable lives, for which they have a
right to be compensated, while the life he
lived was its own best reward.

That life is not perhaps so colourless
and uniform as those of most scholars,
but it is still simple enough and broken
into very simple divisions.   The letters

cover nearly the whole of it, beginning before he was twenty and extending to within a few days of his death. He was born on the 27th of April, 1737 (old style), and died on January 16th, 1794. The period of childhood and education spent at his father's house at Beriton, in a school at Kingston, then at Westminster and Oxford, and finally at Lausanne, occupies the first twenty-one years of his life. He returned from Lausanne in the spring of 1758, and from that time till his father's death in 1770, he lived principally at Beriton, but some part of the year was generally spent in London, and he was abroad from 1763 to 1765. The chief events of this period were the publication of his " Essai sur l'étude de la Littérature " in 1761, and the first conception of his great work. On his father's death in 1770 he became an independent man, and from then till 1783 lived principally in London. During this period, in 1774, he entered Parliament for the nomination borough of Liskeard, and in 1779 he became a Lord of Trade; but the publication of the first volume of the Decline and Fall in 1776, and of the second and third volumes in 1781, are far more important events. Their success decided him to

abandon politics for literature and England
for Switzerland.   He settled at Lausanne
with his friend Deyverdun in September
1783, and there he spent most of the
remaining decade of his life.   He came
to England in August 1787, to see the
concluding volumes of his History through
the press, and stayed a year; and he
came again in the summer of 1793, and
was in London when he died.

There are letters, as I said, covering
nearly the whole of his life; but their tone
and style varies very little.   He is essentially, and far more than most men, the
same personality at nineteen as he is· at
fifty-six; only a little more strenuous and
serious, as was likely enough in an only
child, kept by weak health from his natural
society, and completing his education
in a small Swiss town, at the house of
a Calvinist Minister.   London and the
House of Commons, which he calls "a very
agreeable coffee-house," developed his
lighter side: and the member of White's
and Boodle's takes for a time a good deal
of the fashionable and frivolous tone of
Pall Mall and St. James's.   But the real
Gibbon was more at home in his library
in Bentinck Street; and with the publication of his history, the scholar definitely

gets the upper hand of the man of the world. Not that he returned to the studious severity of his youth. That was not likely, nor even perhaps desirable; for while the boy's horizon was bounded by his books, the man could never entirely forget that he had been a conspicuous figure in fashionable as well as in learned society, or that he had been a member of the English Parliament before he became the historian of the Roman Empire. The result is that there is somewhat more colour and variety in the later letters than in the earlier. But it would be a mistake to look for external interest in Gibbon's letters : their interest belongs to their author, not to the subject of which he treats. He is himself his own most frequent subject and his best. This is so from the very beginning. Take a passage from a letter written to his father when he was only twenty-three. Many sons have written to their fathers to excuse themselves from entering upon an uncongenial career : but most of such compositions would appear very crude by the side of Gibbon's mature criticism of his own character, and of the world it was intended he should enter.

" DEAR SIR,—An address in writing from a person who has the pleasure of being with you every day,

may appear singular. However, I have preferred
this method, as upon paper I can speak without
a blush, and be heard without interruption. . . .
When I first returned to England, attentive to my
future interest, you were so good as to give me
hopes of a seat in Parliament. This seat, according
to the Custom of our venal country, was to be
bought, and fifteen hundred pounds were mentioned
as the price of the purchase. This design flattered
my vanity, as it might enable me to shine in so
august an assembly. It flattered a nobler passion ;
I promised myself that by the means of this seat I
might be one day the instrument of some good to
my country. But I soon perceived how little a
mere virtuous inclination, unassisted by talents,
could contribute towards that great end; and a
very short examination discovered to me that those
talents had not fallen to my lot. Do not, Dear sir,
impute this declaration to a false modesty, the
meanest species of pride. Whatever else I may be
ignorant of, I think I know myself. . . . I shall
say with great truth that I never possessed that
gift of speech, the first requisite of an Orator, which
use and labour may improve, but which nature can
alone bestow. That my temper, quiet, retired, somewhat reserved, could neither acquire popularity,
bear up against opposition, nor mix with ease in
the crowds of public life. That even my genius
(if you will allow me any) is better qualified
for the deliberate compositions of the Closet,
than for the extemporary discourses of the Parliament. An unexpected objection would disconcert
me ; and as I am incapable of explaining to
others what I do not thoroughly understand
myself, I should be meditating, while I ought to
be answering. I even want necessary prejudices
of party, and of nation."

The style is the man, it has been said. Certainly it is so in Gibbon's case. Here is the famous style in all its essentials, making its appearance in a letter written when he was only twenty-three and to his father. No doubt he was a born lover of form, some would say of formality. It is not easy to imagine him receiving his visitors in a dressing-gown : nor were the children of his brain ever allowed to go forth except in full dress. The very fact that he writes, instead of speaking, is characteristic of the man. Everything with him is weighed and premeditated, till it takes an almost judicial tone. And averse as he was to mere correspondence, he says of himself that he never avoided writing a letter of importance. Indeed, one is struck with the industry and energy which led him in those boyish days at Lausanne to despatch long letters on passages in books he was reading to famous scholars with whom he wished to establish an acquaintance. Youthful ambition no doubt often tries to make itself audible to those who are securely seated on the heights it desires to climb : but gods and great men live at ease and do not always heed their suppliants ; and the proof of Gibbon's capacity is that he won not merely attention but respect.

His position, on his return to his father's house, cannot have been very comfortable, particularly from this point of view. No congenial spirit will doubt the truth of his assertion, " I was never less alone than when by myself": but man is a social animal, and few of the species have been more so than Gibbon. At Beriton, however, there were no companions for his mind, and if he had too little of one sort of society, he had too much of another. Family life always has its difficulties for a student: and Gibbon did not fail to experience them.

" By the habit of early rising," he says, " I always secured a sacred portion of the day, and many scattered moments were stolen and employed by my studious industry. But the family hours of breakfast, of dinner, of tea and of supper, were regular and long. After breakfast, Mrs. Gibbon" (his stepmother) " expected my company in her dressing-room; after tea, my father claimed my conversation, and the perusal of the newspapers; and in the midst of an interesting work I was often called down to receive the visit of some idle neighbours. Their dinners and visits required, in due season, a similar return; and I dreaded the period of the full moon, which was usually reserved for our more distant excursions."

Nor had he any agricultural or sporting

tastes to make the country more attractive to him.

"My father could never inspire me with his love and knowledge of farming. I never handled a gun, I seldom mounted a horse; and my philosophic walks were soon terminated by a shady bench, where I was long detained by the sedentary amusement of reading or meditation."

Sport, indeed, was not treated nearly so seriously a hundred years ago as it is now. No one now ventures to speak disrespectfully of it; then polite as well as political circles could join in Addison's laugh at the Tory fox-hunter; and Chesterfield, the supreme man of the world and of society, could write: "*mange du gibier si tu veux: mais ne sois pas ton propre boucher.*" Gibbon's tone is less severe but not less contemptuous: "Clarke, who is writing near me," he says in one letter, "begs to be remembered; the savage is going to hunt Foxes in Northamptonshire"; and in another he gives a brief and crushing account of the society at a country house: "I found Lord Egremont and fourscore fox-hounds." Naturally enough, with such tastes he did not love the country, never went there till he was obliged, and stayed indoors when he did. "Never pretend to allure me," he writes to Lord Sheffield, "by painting in odious colours the dust of London. I love the dust, and whenever I move into the Wold, it is to visit you and My lady, and not your Trees." He complains to Mrs. Gibbon of "this abominable fine weather," which drives him out from "my own new clean comfortable dear house, which I like better every week I pass in it. . . . If it would but rain, I should enjoy that unity of study and society, in which I have always placed my prospect of happiness." Summer he considered the most uncomfortable of all seasons, because it tempted people to go out; and bore a grudge against it for forcing him to leave London. "I shall probably defer my Derbyshire Journey till another year," he says in a letter to Lord Sheffield; "sufficient for the summer is the evil thereof, of one distant country Excursion."

Altogether he must have been very glad when, after long delays of business caused by his father's death, he could at last establish himself permanently in London. He gives us some pictures of his life there. The mornings were given to his library ("I hate to go out in the morning," he says): the afternoons and evenings to the House when it was sitting, or to dinners

and suppers and society. He must, however, have worked harder than he allows;
for it was not till October 1772, that he
" abjured the rustic deities of Beriton, and
reconciled himself to the Catholic Church
of London," and the first volume of the
Decline and Fall appeared in February
1776. But he was never a hermit, and
least of all at this period of his life. He
paid a visit of several months to Paris in
1777, and this is how he lived:

"I lead a very agreeable life; let me just condescend to observe, that it is not extravagant.
After decking myself out with silks and silver,
the ordinary establishment of Coach, Lodgeing,
Servants, eating, and pocket expences, does not
exceed sixty pounds pr. month. Yet I have two
footmen in handsome liveries behind my Coach,
and my apartment is hung with damask. . . .

"Let me just in two words give you an idea of
my day. I am now going (nine o'clock) to the
King's Library, where I shall stay till twelve. As
soon as I am dressed I set out to dine with the
Duke de Nivernois; shall go from thence to the
French Comedy into the Princess de Beauvau's
loge grillée, and am not quite determined whether
I shall sup at Madame du Deffand's, Madame
Necker's, or the Sardinian Embassadress's."

After the two footmen and the Duke
and the Princess, one is surprised at the
survival of the three hours in the Library;
but the taste for the *loge grillée* and that

for a Greek or Latin folio were equally
real in Gibbon ; and the indulgence of the
one probably produced a keener appetite
for the other. He never gave himself
more absolutely to his studies than he did
as a boy at Lausanne ; but his absorption
in higher matters did not even then render
him insensible to the loss of "the indispensable comfort of a servant."   All
through his life he enjoyed, and never
refused himself, a temperate indulgence
in the pleasures of the table.   During an
August in London, he would not be alone,
but found out new friends and acquaintances to visit, gave "the prettiest little
dinners in the world," and congratulates
himself that by this means "the monster
Ennui preserves a respectful distance."

Everyone knows the famous declaration
of his later life ; "good Madeira is now
become essential to my health and reputation." He was very much in earnest
about it, and often mentions it to Lord
Sheffield : "pray take serious strenuous
measures for sending me a pipe of excellent Madeira." When estimating in a
French letter to Deyverdun, the expense
of his proposed settlement at Lausanne,
his household plans include "a little table
for two epicurean philosophers, four, five,

or six servants, friends pretty often, feasts pretty rarely, much enjoyment and little luxury." Indeed, as he grows older, he does not cease to be a disciple of Epicurus, but his discipleship becomes more and more prudent and temperate. We hear of no more participations, as once at Boodle's, in masquerades costing two thousand guineas in a single evening. With the settlement at Lausanne the scholar and philosopher in him became more and more dominant. There is still plenty of society; but life grows simpler and more regular, the few real friendships deepen, the miscellaneous acquaintances gradually disappear. Here is his account of his day at Lausanne; it was sent soon after he went there to that " Aunt Kitty " who had been more than a mother to him:

"In this season" (the date is December 27th) "I rise a little before eight; at nine I am called from my study to breakfast, which I always perform alone, in the English style; and, with the aid of Caplin,[1] I perceive no difference between Lausanne and Bentinck-Street. Our mornings are usually passed in separate studies; we never approach each other's door without a previous message, or thrice knocking, and my apartment is already sacred and formidable to strangers. I dress at half-past one, and at two (an early hour, to which I am not

[1] His English valet.

perfectly reconciled) we sit down to dinner. We have hired a female cook, well skilled in her profession, and accustomed to the taste of every nation; as, for instance, we had excellent mince-pies yesterday. After dinner and the departure of our company, one, two, or three friends, we read together some amusing book, or play at chess, or retire to our rooms, or make visits, or go to the coffee-house. Between six and seven the assemblies begin, and I am oppressed only with their number and variety. Whist, at shillings or half-crowns, is the game I generally play, and I play three rubbers with pleasure. Between nine and ten we withdraw to our bread and cheese, and friendly converse, which sends us to bed at eleven; but these sober hours are too often interrupted by private or numerous suppers, which I have not the courage to resist, though I practice a laudable abstinence at the best furnished tables."

The picture of studious and social felicity does not conclude without the optimistic touch, true enough most likely, but amusingly characteristic of the complacent vanity natural to a middle-aged bachelor, who is at once a beau and a wit: "if I do not deceive myself, and if Deyverdun does not flatter me, I am already a general favourite." Never certainly had man, and least of all, I am afraid, man of letters, a more equable, contented, reasonable disposition. "I have seriously resumed," he says in 1784, "the prosecution of my history; each day and each month adds something to the completion of the great work. The progress is slow, the labour continual, and the end remote and uncertain. Yet every day brings its amusement as well as labour." And in his serene self-satisfaction, he is not afraid to conclude: "with health and competence, a full independence of mind and action, a delightful habitation, a true friend, and many pleasant acquaintances, you will allow that I am rather an object of envy than pity."

For a temperament of this sort, life contains no disappointments. Nothing is desired that is not attainable: nothing attempted that is not accomplished. The triumphant execution of the gigantic scheme of his history was due as much to his cheerful temper as to his genius or industry.

No doubt he was exceptionally lucky in the matter of freedom from cares and worries. But, as a great moralist said, "if you would have anything good, receive it from yourself." Some people upset themselves about every trifle that goes wrong. Gibbon owed most of his serenity to his own good sense. It was annoying, no doubt, that the stocks fell, or that

Beriton could not be sold : but it was no more : he disdained to allow such matters to seriously interfere either with his occupations or his cheerfulness. It is true that he had Lord Sheffield to manage his business affairs for him ; but there are plenty of people who make their friends do their business, but reserve the privilege of incessantly complaining of the result. Gibbon, as we now know, took a rational interest in his affairs, and placed his plenipotentiary in full and frequent possession of his views. But, as to the final decision, he nearly always left Lord Sheffield a free hand : and the instructions which he had once given, he never recalled.

Their friendship is a striking instance of the mutual attraction of contrary tastes. Lord Sheffield was a man for whom the multiplication of business was the great pleasure of life. Gibbon was a poet in his detestation of business, if in nothing else. When he has to write about it he confesses "I shove the ugly monster to the end of this epistle and will confine him to a page by himself, that he may not infect the purer air of our correspondence." Again and again he leaves letters, which he suspects to have the taint of business

about them, lying days or weeks unopened.
" I have a letter from Hugonin," he tells
Lord Sheffield, "a *dreadful* one I believe,
but it has lain four days unperused in my
drawers.   Let me turn it over to you."
He would "much rather pass the time in
a horse-pond and still rather in his library
with the Decline and Fall," than in
accompanying his friend and a solicitor in
an examination of Beriton with a view
to its sale.   And when he bids " without
regret, an everlasting farewell" to the
House of Commons, he says, " the agreeable hour of five o'Clock in the morning,
at which you commonly retire, does not
tend to revive my attachment ; but if you
add the soft hours of your morning com-
mittee, in the discussion of taxes, customs,
frauds, smugglers, etc., I think I should
beg to be released and quietly sent to the
Gallies as a place of leisure and freedom.
Yet I do not depart from my general
principles of toleration ;   some animals
are made to live in the water, others on
the Earth, many in the air, and some, as
it is now believed, even in fire."

His has been called a Pagan, especially
a Roman, character ;   and there is a good
deal of rather obvious truth in the remark.
There were probably few English country

houses in which he felt as much at home,
as he would have felt at one of Cicero's or
Seneca's villas.   But, just as it would be
an immense mistake to think of him as a
mere epicure, because no house would
have suited him that did not contain a
dining-room and a drawing-room, as well
as a library and a study, it would be
almost equally absurd to fancy he had no
heart because he knew nothing of the
peculiarly Christian sentiments like the
" enthusiasm of humanity."   His friends
did not find it so.   When the fox-hunting
Godfrey Clarke lost his father, Gibbon
was the only person he wished to see
except his own family; and to his father,
his stepmother, his aunt, and his few
friends, he was all that a son, a nephew,
or a friend can be.   He sacrificed not
merely his leisure and his tastes, but
something of his prospects and fortune,
to gratify a father who had not thought
too much of his son's interests; for Mrs.
Gibbon he showed the practical and
unselfish nature of his regard by a perfectly voluntary increase of her jointure
and by making it his first care in dealing
with his property that every reasonable
or unreasonable wish of hers should be
carried out; and for " Aunt Kitty," whose

life and ways and character lay so very
far from his, he proved the genuineness
of his affection by a hundred little acts of
kindness, only one or two of which, indeed,
have come down to us, but they are
enough to assure us of the reality of the
rest. Gibbon had not much of what
we call "soul," no doubt; indeed, he
may be said to have gone through life in
the most complete unconsciousness of
all its highest and most spiritual possibilities: still, only a man who had real
depth of heart, would have thought, as he
did, of asking that "Aunt Kitty," when
she went to Sheffield Place, might sleep
in the room in which he usually slept.
There is a touch of tenderness in that
little act of thoughtfulness, and a touch
of insight into an old maid's simple
fancies, which, to tell the truth, one
would hardly have suspected in Gibbon.
But even if it stood more absolutely alone
in our knowledge of him than it does, it
is impossible to believe that it stood alone
in fact. His somewhat reserved and
formal nature probably did not allow him
to speak the language of the heart very
easily; and his heart may, perhaps, have
had much to say which it found no words
to express. Still, at times he does give

us glimpses of this side of his nature: whether they are more than glimpses we can hardly say. One of his brother officers in the militia dies, and he writes to Lord Sheffield: "You will excuse my having said so much of a man you had not the least knowledge of: but my mind is just now so very full of him that I cannot easily talk, or even think, of anything else." His father is ill, and he tells the same friend, "that the same event appears in a very different light when the danger is serious and immediate; or, when in the gaiety of a tavern dinner, we affect an insensibility that would do us no great honour were it real." He writes to Lady Sheffield from Lausanne: "Adieu. I feel every day that the distance serves only to make me think with more tenderness of the persons whom I love": and when she died, in 1793, at the height of the revolutionary ferment, he left Lausanne at once in spite of distance, difficulties, and even some danger, to give his friend the comfort of his presence. There is heart, too, behind the rather stilted language of the letter he wrote on receiving the news.

"My Dearest Friend, for such you most truly are, nor does there exist a person who obtains, or shall ever obtain, a superior place in my esteem and affection.

"After too long a silence I was sitting down to write, when, only yesterday morning (such is now the irregular slowness of the English post) I was suddenly struck, indeed struck to the heart, by the fatal intelligence from Sir Henry Clinton and M. de Lally. Alas! what is life, and what are our hopes and projects! When I embraced her at your departure from Lausanne, could I imagine that it was for the last time? When I postponed to another summer my journey to England, could I apprehend that I never, never should see her again? I have often deplored the nervous complaints which so deeply affected her happiness and spirits, but I always hoped that she would spin her feeble thread to a long duration, and that her delicate frame would survive (as is often the case) many constitutions of a stouter appearance. In four days! In your absence, in that of her children! But she is now at rest; and if there be a future state, her mild virtues have surely entitled her to the reward of pure and perfect felicity. It is for you that I feel; and I can judge of your sentiments by comparing them with my own. I have lost, it is true, an amiable and affectionate friend, whom I had known and loved above three and twenty years, and whom I often styled by the endearing name of sister. But you are deprived of the companion of your life, the wife of your choice, and the mother of your children—poor children!"

A week later, the day before he started for England, he writes again. He has heard nothing further, and is in terrible anxiety about his friend:

"I am left in a state of darkness to the workings of my own fancy, which imagines everything that is sad and shocking. What can I think of for your relief and comfort? I will not expatiate on those commonplace topics, which have never dried a single tear; but let me advise, let me urge, you to force yourself into business, as I would try to force myself into study. The mind must not be idle; if it be not exercised on external objects, it will prey on its own vitals."

No one will claim for Gibbon that he possessed an exceptionally affectionate nature, but the man who wrote these letters was not a heartless man. And if overflowings of the heart are somewhat rare with him, there is this, at least, to be said in his excuse. Human sympathies need the natural human relationships for their development; and Gibbon hardly remembered his mother, lost his brothers and sisters in their infancy, and had no wife or child. During the twenty-three years between his father's death and his own, he lived chiefly alone; and solitude is certainly the school of selfishness. A man feels that it is absurd not to consult his own convenience when there is no one else's to consult; and so, indeed, it is. But there is danger in it; for a man who lives alone is consulting his own convenience so often that he is apt to forget how to consult anything else. The affection felt for Gibbon all through, and in spite of long separations, by his step-mother and his aunt, by Lord Sheffield and his whole family, and by Deyverdun and the de Sévery's at Lausanne, is sufficient proof that he rose above this besetting temptation of the bachelor.

He seems never, at least in mature life, to have seriously contemplated emerging from his solitude by the natural road of marriage. He and his friend Deyverdun, did, indeed, agree that a house like theirs would be "regulated and graced and enlivened by an agreeable female Companion," but "each of us," Gibbon says, "seems desirous that his friend should sacrifice himself for the public good." When Deyverdun died, the idea again entered his mind; but, as he characteristically and most justly remarks, "the choice is difficult, the success doubtful, the engagement perpetual," and he contented himself with his "mistress, Fanny Lausanne." Nor, except for his short-lived parliamentary ambitions, does he ever seem to have thought of any career but that of a scholar, and, though Mrs. Gibbon, "with seeming wisdom," exhorted him to take chambers in the Temple and read for the Bar, he does not repent of having neglected her advice. " Few men," as he says, " without the spur of necessity, have resolution to force their way through the thorns and thickets of that gloomy labyrinth. Nature had not endowed me with the bold and ready eloquence which makes itself heard amidst the tumult of the Bar; and I should probably have been diverted from the labours of literature, without acquiring the fame or fortune of a successful pleader. I had no need to call to my aid the regular duties of a profession; every day, every hour was agreeably filled; nor have I known, like so many of my countrymen, the tediousness of an idle life."

The words take us back to what is after all the central thing about him, the rare definiteness with which he saw his goal, and the union of cheerfulness and determination, almost equally rare, with which he pursued it. He was one of those happiest of mortals who do not need the " preponderance from without," for whose guidance Wilhelm Meister longed; for him the preponderance within spoke clear enough. The call to be a scholar was

in him from the first, the special call to
history came later.   Both were promptly,
strenuously, unwearyingly obeyed ; and to
that cheerful and long-sustained obedience
the historian owed one of the happiest of
lives, and we owe the greatest work of
history in a modern language.

CHARLES LAMB.[1]

Lamb is, perhaps, the only letter-writer who has ever been overpraised. Strong things have been said about Cowper and Edward FitzGerald, and, of course, about Madame de Sévigné : but, then, the facts are stronger still. Their letters are perfect, or not far away from being so, and you never can express perfection. Charles Lamb's have often received the same sort of praise. I confess that this seems to me a mistake. They are easy, humorous, witty, interesting; altogether delightful reading : but the charm of FitzGerald, of Cowper, that is just what it seems to me they have not quite got. There are two reasons for this. One, which may be the less important, is that Lamb, justly dear as he was to his friends, and will always be to his readers, was evidently not a man of generally attractive personality. No one, I suppose, ever came into close contact

[1] The best edition of Lamb's Letters is that of Canon Ainger, in two volumes, Macmillan, 1888 ; reprinted 1897.

with Cowper without loving that beautiful character. The man who knew Fitz-Gerald and did not like him has yet to be found. But it is plain that good judges who met Lamb, people who ought to have liked him, carried away an unpleasant impression of him. This is explained by his shyness; but who could be shyer than FitzGerald, or Cowper, or Gray? The truth is, that the shyness which leads to awkward silence is one thing, and the shyness which leads to drinking too much and forcing unacceptable jokes on the company is another, and that they necessarily make quite different impressions on a casual stranger. The reader of letters is, partly, in the position of the casual stranger. He sees, what no stranger sees, the intimate and beautiful side of Lamb's nature: but he also sees what all see, and what is also very real, the man's grosser, unattractive side. There is no need for him to judge Lamb, who is, indeed, almost certain, with his heroic unselfishness, to be in the essential part of morals far away above any level his reader has attained to. But he is not bound to close his eyes to facts: and he cannot but see and feel that there is an unpleasant element in Lamb, which had its effect on his contemporaries, and cannot but have it on his readers. Lamb was a little wanting, in fact, in that fine quality of self-restraint, which is the essential characteristic of a gentleman, and to which, where it exists, the unfortunate failing of which Lamb was a victim, is specially fatal. We will not dare to condemn him, the man of terrible sorrows and of the terrible temptations which they bring, on account of a vice so common in his day; only the fact remains that a friend with that failing cannot be what he might have been without it. Still less can we blame Lamb, the son of a barrister's servant, for being without that perfect good taste in matters of conduct and social intercourse, which was inherited as a birthright by Cowper and FitzGerald (however carelessly the latter might now and then choose to throw it away), and came to Gray, the tradesman's son, it may be by some divine good fortune, or more simply, perhaps, as the result of the forming influences of the first of schools and the second of Universities.

The other reason why Lamb's letters cannot carry with them the charm of these others, lies in his literary habit and manner. What is a letter? It is written talk, with something, but not all, of the easiness of talking, and something, not all, of the formality of writing. It is at once spontaneous and deliberate, a thing of art and a thing of amusement, the idle occupation of an hour, and the sure index of a character. It must not be all serious, for then it ought to have been an essay or a book; it must not be all trifles, for then it will not have deserved ink and paper. But the most essential of all its qualities are its spontaneity, and, so to speak, its personality. The two sorts of letters which are intolerable are the laboured sort and the sort which may be called the " epistle general." No art is so bound to conceal itself as the art of letter-writing; and, though personality may be said, in one sense, to be the salt of all literature, there is none which calls for it so unmistakeably as the letter. These two points are vital. A letter, indeed, will not be literature unless it be written according to the rules of the art of writing; but, unless it flow spontaneously from the writer's mind and pen, unless, too, it be *from* him and no one else, *to* his correspondent and no one else, it not only will not be literature, it will not be a real letter at all. Now Lamb's letters are weak in both these points.

They are too much alike, wanting the play of varied personality which we get, for instance, in the comparison of Gray writing to West, and the same Gray writing to Bonstetten. This is, however, the smaller matter of the two. The real defect of Lamb's letters, I make bold to say, is their want of spontaneity. It can hardly be illustrated in an essay of this sort, for it is only felt when they are read as a whole. It does not strike one in two letters, or ten or twenty; but read the whole of one of Canon Ainger's volumes, and, charming as so much of it is, there gradually arises a sense of something artificial which fatigues the mind. Lamb plays delightfully in them, it is true, but it is too often the play of a man who has set himself to amuse the company. One is conscious of him feeling about for a subject, finding it, and then artistically making the best of it. It is often admirable fooling, with admirable seriousness thrown in, too, very likely; but it is too often also a professed essayist working out a set theme. To vary his own admirable phrase about Wordsworth's moralities, what he says does not give the impression of "sliding into the mind of the writer while he was imagining no such matter." Letter after letter, with its deliberate archaisms of language and spelling, with its far-fetched quaintness of thought and image, suggests something of the conscious humourist acting up to his part. When one has read thirty or forty of them, it is impossible to avoid a certain sensation that Lamb is just a little inclined to pose. No doubt there never was a man into whose head all oddities, new and old, came so freely, so naturally; but was there ever a man to whom it was perfectly natural to begin a letter, " Dear Fugueist, or hear'st thou rather contrapuntist " ? Or, " Saturday, 25th of July, A.D. 1829, 11 A.M. There! a fuller, plumper, juicier date never dropt from Idumean palm. Am I in the *date*-ive case now ? If not, a fig for dates, which is more than a date is worth." Fooling of this kind is well enough once in a while, but incessantly, perpetually, as a matter of course! How inferior to the careless humour of FitzGerald! The one man never quite gets away from the professed writer, who had supplied his tale of jokes to the *Morning Post*, and his monthly essay to the magazines. The other writes all the better for having no writership to get away from. Lamb, at his worst, writes as a task, " loath," as

he himself says, " to throw away composition, the Magazine paying me so much
a page." At these times he is like a very
clever undergraduate essayist or a sixteenth century poet, festooning some set
theme with flowers of assent and illustra-
tion, or torturing it with thorns of para-
doxical contradiction. The happiness, on
the other hand, of such a man as Fitz-
Gerald is that he writes when and as he
pleases, raising no expectations of wit
and disappointing none, hampered by no
habit of journalism, by no established
reputation, with no thought but of his
friends and himself, with no subject but
their doings and his own.

One is glad to have done with so ungracious a business as criticising a man
we love so well as Lamb. It would not
have been necessary if he had not suffered
from the unkindness of extravagant praise.
But, the protest once made, I gladly pass
to the pleasant business of seeing Lamb
and his letters no longer in the special
light of comparisons, but as they are in
and for themselves.

" A fig for dates " is his own cry, but
it may be that some reader of more exact
or more exacting character will be glad
to be reminded just of his birth and death,

and the one or two other landmarks of his life. One moves more comfortably in the wandering flux of impressions that float round a man, if one has a date or two to guide the course by. Lamb was born in 1775, his father being John Lamb, clerk and servant to a Bencher of the Inner Temple. In 1782, he went to Christ's Hospital, where he began his friendship with Coleridge. About ten years later he became a clerk in the service of the East India Company, at their house in Leadenhall Street, where he remained till 1825. It was in September, 1796, that the great tragedy which over-shadowed his life occurred : his sister Mary, in a moment of madness, killing her mother and wounding her father. Lamb at once made it his duty to save his sister from an asylum, arranged for her lodging till his father died, and then took her to live with him, which she did for the rest of his life, though usually obliged by her attacks to spend a month or two of every year away from him under special treatment. In 1797, he published poems jointly with Coleridge and Lloyd. In 1801, he and his sister went to live in Mitre Court, overlooking King's Bench Walk. At this time he wrote for the *Morning Post* and other papers. In 1802

he printed his play "John Woodvil."
"Tales from Shakspeare" appeared in
1807, and the "Specimens of Dramatic
Poets" in 1808.   In 1817, the brother
and sister left the Temple, where they
had lived since 1801 (though not all the
time in the same rooms), and went to
Great Russell Street.   In 1818, Ollier
published Lamb's works in two volumes.
In 1820, the *London Magazine* began, and
in it the "Essays of Elia," the first
collected series of which was published in
1823.   In the same year Lamb and his
sister adopted Emma Isola, who was afterwards Mrs. Moxon.   In 1825 he retired
on a pension of £440, and during the rest
of his life was settled with his sister at
various places, Enfield and Edmonton
among others, till he died on the 27th of
December, 1834.   His sister survived, in
increasing mental weakness, till 1847.

Lamb is remembered, it may be said,
in four characters.   He is one of the
few literary critics whose criticism has
definitely achieved immortality ; and
though his humour, like his criticism,
moves in a narrow field, it is certain
that neither Mrs. Battle nor the Poor
Relations can ever die.   Then he has a
unique place in our affections as the

tenderest and most devoted of brothers. And for the ever-increasing army of Londoners, he is the man who loved London as no one else ever did, and who told his love. All these things are in his letters, worth the finding.

Take his love of London first. Has anyone ever praised London as he did? Johnson may have pronounced in his hearty, magisterial way that the man who is tired of London is tired of life, may have smacked his lips over the fine variety of meats it provided for his intellectual palate, may have delighted in its "full tide of human existence" at Charing Cross. But for the place itself, for its streets and buildings, he cared nothing. And his affection was not of Lamb's sort, that delights to linger and play with every stone in the Temple or Covent Garden, like an old man fondling his grandchildren. Johnson's London is his most valued and interesting acquaintance. Lamb's London is the companion of his youth, the mistress of his bosom, the favourite child of his old age. London is for him an "enchanting (more than Mahometan) paradise, whose dirtiest drab-frequented alley, and her lowest bowing tradesman, I would not exchange for Skiddaw, Helvellyn, James, Walter, and the parson into the bargain." Hear him break out in her praise to Wordsworth, when he had only known her twenty-five years :—

"I have passed all my days in London until I have formed as many and intense local attachments as any of you mountaineers can have done with dead Nature. The lighted shops of the Strand and Fleet Street; the innumerable trades, tradesmen, and customers, coaches, waggons, playhouses; all the bustle and wickedness round about Covent Garden : the very women of the town : the watchmen, drunken scenes, rattles ; life awake, if you awake, at all hours of the night ; the impossibility of being dull in Fleet Street ; the crowds, the very dirt and mud, the sun shining upon houses and pavements, the print-shops, the old bookstalls, parsons cheapening books, coffee-houses, steams of soups from kitchens, the pantomimes—London itself a pantomime and a masquerade—all these things work themselves into my mind and feed me, without a power of satiating me. The wonder of these sights impels me into night-walks about her crowded streets, and I often shed tears in the motley Strand from fulness of joy at so much life."

It is strange to have to go to the New World for a parallel to Lamb, oldest-fashioned of men, whose very swaddling clothes one would look to find of the pattern of Burton's day or Massinger's. Yet there is one man, and only one, in all literature whom this outburst at once calls up. What can be more exactly the manner of Walt Whitman, his best manner, than this wonderful catalogue ? "The very women of the town," "life awake *if you awake*," "the impossibility of being dull in Fleet Street," "the pantomimes—*London itself a pantomime*" : it is the very voice, almost the very trick of accent of the poet of Brooklyn Ferry! Nor are these things mere catalogues, as is sometimes said. They pant and beat with the pulse of a living personality. And the kinship is as close in matter as in manner. Who but Lamb and Whitman have been able to forget so utterly as this the petty miseries that belong to a great city's noise and crowds, and take such exultant, throbbing delight in the infinite variety and energy of its life ? The poetry of the streets can never, perhaps, be as high and pure as that of the mountains, but the eye that discovers it is a still rarer gift.

Young or old, in leisure and in business, in London or out of it, Lamb's taste never changed. Four years before he died he writes from Enfield to Barton, the Quaker Poet :—

" Let me congratulate you on the Spring coming in, and do you in return condole with me on the Winter going out. I dread the prospects of Summer, with his all-day-long days. No need of his assistance to make country places dull. With fire and candle-light I can dream myself in Holborn. . . . Give me old London at fire and plague times, rather than these tepid gales, healthy country air and purposeless exercise."

A year before his death " London streets and faces," when he sees them, still "cheer me inexpressibly!" And to Wordsworth, to whom his playful malice specially loves to address its London hymns and panegyrics, he cries from Enfield :—

"O let no native Londoner imagine that health, and rest, and innocent occupation, interchange of converse sweet, and recreative study, can make the country anything better than altogether odious and detestable! A garden was the primitive prison, till man, with Promethean felicity and boldness, luckily sinned himself out of it. Thence followed Babylon, Nineveh, Venice, London, haberdashers, goldsmiths, taverns, playhouses, satires, epigrams, puns—these all came in on the town part, and the thither side of innocence."

A man who can write like this will be believed whatever he says ; but then, so will FitzGerald, when he writes from Charlotte Street to Lamb's own Barton—

"Oh, Barton man! but I am grilled here. Oh, for to sit upon the banks of the dear old Deben, with the worthy collier sloop going forth into the wide world as the sun sinks!"

Or to Frederick Tennyson, from Boulge—

"I read of mornings: the same old books over and over again, having no command of new ones; walk with my great black dog of an afternoon, and at evening sit with open windows, up to which China roses climb, with my pipe, while the blackbirds and thrushes begin to rustle bedwards in the garden, and the nightingale to have the neighbourhood to herself."

We are weak creatures in the presence of these magicians! Call it prose or poetry, poetry in prose, or what you will, so long as the echo of the enchanter's voice is in our ears, we love and hate, believe and feel as he does, are Londoners with Lamb, set Paradise in Suffolk with Edward Fitz-Gerald!

Yet it must not be thought that Lamb was totally insensible to the beauty of nature, even on its grander side. He had little chance of seeing it, but when he did, as in his visit to Coleridge at Keswick, he admits having "satisfied himself that there is such a thing as that which tourists call *romantic*": is enthusiastic over the evening in Coleridge's study, "looking out upon the last fading view of Skiddaw, and his broad-breasted brethren: what a night!", and declares that the day he went up Skiddaw "will stand out like a mountain" in his life. Still, even then, with the memory of the vision fresh upon him, he is not afraid to tell Wordsworth that "Fleet Street and the Strand are better places to live in." London never had on him the effect which it has on most cultivated men, who find themselves every year more utterly outdoing their country contemporaries in delighted consciousness of Nature, simple or sublime. On him the great city cast a spell continuous and unbroken, admitting no reaction ; instead of sending him to the fields, it drew its own mantle ever more and more closely about his eyes and affections, and kept him more entirely to itself.

Lamb's literary criticism ranks with his wonderful management of the essay as a vehicle for depicting and criticising human life, and with his peculiar humour, as the basis of his permanent fame. I have nothing to say here of the " Tragedies of Shakespeare" and the rest; but we may trace the same fine vein of criticism everywhere in the letters. He was not a profound critic like Coleridge ; it was not in the nature of his mind to soar very high above the surface of things, or to penetrate very far below it. In fact, he was rather a man of taste than a man of genius. Nor was his taste the fine catholic taste of such a critic as Matthew Arnold. That was impossible; for Greek, French, German, Spanish, were closed books to him, and his Italian was of the scantiest. I know no evidence that he cared to read the Latin poets after he left school. But within certain rather narrow limitations his taste is astonishingly sure. What these limitations were no one has pointed out better than himself. He is thanking Southey for " Roderick," and takes occasion to say that he prefers it to "Kehama," because his imagination is so soon out of its depth in such vast subjects. That is just the fact about him, as may be seen, for instance, in his incapacity to appreciate "Faust." He describes himself admirably :—

" My imagination goes sinking and floundering in the vast spaces of unopened-before systems and faiths; I am put out of the pale of my old sympathies; my moral sense is almost outraged; I can't believe—or, with horror, am made to believe — such desperate chances against Omnipotence, such disturbances of faith to the centre; the more potent, the more painful the spell. Jove and his brotherhood of gods, tottering with the giant assailings, I can bear, for the soul's hopes are not struck at in such contests; but your Oriental almighties are too much types of the intangible prototype to be meddled with without shuddering. . . . I have a timid imagination, I am afraid. I do not willingly admit of strange beliefs, or out-of-the-way creeds or places. I never read books of travels, at least not farther than Paris or Rome. I can just endure Moors, because of their connection as foes with Christians; but Abyssinians, Ethiops, Esquimaux, Dervises, and all that tribe, I hate. . . . I am a Christian, Englishman, Londoner, *Templar*. God help me when I come to put off these snug relations, and to get abroad into the world to come!"

We may even go farther than he does. He is a Christian, who cares nothing for creeds, and too little for some important points of practice : an Englishman, who lived through the great war without being aware, apparently, that anything of the kind was going on : a Londoner, who detested business ; and a Templar, who knew nothing of law. His range of time and thought is equally narrow. He did not go behind the Tudor dawn of civilisation, nor look farther than the gospel that issued from the Lakes. " I have not a black-letter book among mine, old Chaucer excepted," he writes to Harrison Ains-worth, " and am not bibliomanist enough to like black-letter." He adds his sensible and conclusive reason ; " it is painful to read." In his own day, he cares for little outside his own circle. In the cases of Byron and Shelley, for instance, his critical faculty shows itself in his swift detection of their weak spots ; for the rest he has no eye. Byron is " great in so little a way. To be a Poet is to be the Man, not a petty portion of occasional low passion worked up in a permanent form of humanity." The news from Missolonghi does not move him.

" He was to me offensive, and I never can make out his great *power* which his admirers talk of. Why, a line of Wordsworth's is a lever to lift the immortal spirit ! Byron can only move the Spleen. He was at best a Satyrist—in any other way, he was mean enough. I daresay I do him injustice ; but I cannot love him, nor squeeze a tear to his memory."

Lack of ideas and serious thought, a pose of boredom, a certain atmosphere of the clubs and the man about town ; these might be the headings to-day of a chapter on Byron's weak points ; and Lamb has seen them all. He has even seen that Don Juan is a greater work than Childe Harold. But such greatness as Childe Harold really has, he has not seen. He fails even more completely to see the greatness of Shelley, even quoting with approval Hazlitt's amazing utterance, " Many are the wiser and better for reading Shakespeare ; but nobody was ever wiser or better for reading Shelley." It would be difficult to make a more unfortunate remark about the poet who probably ranks next after Milton and Wordsworth in this matter of "making people better." But Lamb hits exactly in a sentence on Shelley's real weakness as he did on Byron's—

"For his theories and nostrums, they are oracular enough, . . . but, for the most part, ringing with their own emptiness."

Nothing better has ever been said about that side of Shelley, whose thought has proved as unsubstantial and barren as his emotion has shown itself true and inspiring. Keats Lamb never even mentions. One is pleased to find him writing to Landor that "Rose Aylmer" has "a charm I cannot explain—I have lived upon it for weeks." What Lamb cared for more than any other thing on printed paper was finely managed language dealing with the common human emotions, and of that "Rose Aylmer" is an absolutely perfect example. It is more surprising to come across his unhesitating recognition of Blake's gifts, both as painter and poet. After all, perhaps, the man who lives for weeks upon "Rose Aylmer," who knows without any telling, though he cannot quote it correctly, that—

"Tiger, tiger burning bright
Thro' the desarts of the night,"

is "glorious," and says at first reading of Wordsworth's "But thou that didst appear so fair," that "no lovelier stanza can be found in the wide world of poetry," has some critical triumphs to set against any blindness in the matter of Byron, Keats, and Shelley. Besides, necessary as it is to take a critic's breadth or narrowness of range into account in attempting to fix his rank, it is still more necessary to consider the quality of his work within his own field, whether it be large or small. And there is no doubt about the quality of Lamb's. Of English books written between 1550 and 1700, and of the work of the great men with whom accident and intellectual sympathy had once united him, he is that rarest of things, a discriminating enthusiast. It may be that the enthusiasm is unduly conspicuous in the case of the old folios, as the discrimination is, perhaps, in that of the living friends; but they are both there in both cases. No one has ever said so many things that stick in the memory about the old writers. The talk about books which is remembered is that which is at once true and personal, truth ringing with the echo, perhaps with the emotion, of individual experience. That is what we get when we hear Lamb say that the "graceful rambling" of Cowley's Essays is "delicious"; or that "Chapman is divine"; or that Fuller is a "dear, fine, silly old angel"; or, again, when he says of Burnet's "History":—

"Did you ever read that garrulous, pleasant history? He tells his story like an old man past political service, bragging to his sons on winter evenings of the part he took in public transactions, when his 'old cap was new.' Full of scandal, which all true history is. No palliatives: but all the stark wickedness, that actually gives the *momentum* to national actors. Quite the prattle of age and outlived importance. Truth and sincerity staring out upon you perpetually in *alto relievo*. Himself a party man—he makes you a party man. None of the cursed philosophical Humeian indifference, so cold, and unnatural, and inhuman! None of the cursed Gibbonian fine writing, so fine and composite. None of Dr. Robertson's periods with three members. None of Mr. Roscoe's sage remarks, all so apposite, and coming in so clever, lest the reader should have had the trouble of drawing an inference. Burnet's good old prattle I can bring present to my mind: I can make the revolution present to me: the French revolution, by a converse perversity in my nature, I fling as far *from* me."

Here is assuredly not the whole truth, but one side of it, put to perfection once for all with the "perversity" of genius. And he is not always unable, even when his feelings are strongest, to keep himself within the park palings of strictest truth.

Every word of what he says of Cervantes is a naked fact. "Quixote is the very depository and treasury of chivalry and highest notions." Yet how personal it is! How many Englishmen in Lamb's day had discovered anything but food for laughter in those immortal adventures? No book, again, ever had the right thing said so perfectly about it as the "Complete Angler" had in Lamb's two sentences: "It breathes the very spirit of innocence, purity, and simplicity of heart. . . . It would sweeten a man's temper at any time to read it : it would Christianise every discordant angry passion." We all feel a little of this to-day; but it was Lamb who gave us back these lost ancients. He is the real editor of all the good reprints which are among the things of happiest augury in the publishers' announcements of to-day. His love for old books was such that it even sometimes carried him behind the 1550 limit I have mentioned. Here is a story too characteristic to be omitted:—

"I have just come from town, where I have been to get my bit of quarterly pension: and have brought home, from stalls in Barbican, the old 'Pilgrim's Progress' with the prints—Vanity Fair, etc.—now scarce. Four shillings. Cheap. And also one of whom I have oft heard and had dreams,

but never saw in the flesh—that is in sheepskin—
' The whole theologic works of THOMAS AQUINAS.'
My arms ached with lugging it a mile to the
stage ; but the burden was a pleasure, such as old
Anchises was to the shoulders of Æneas, or the
Lady to the Lover in old romance, who having to
carry her to the top of a high mountain (the price
of obtaining her), clambered with her to the top,
and fell dead with fatigue.

' Oh, the glorious old Schoolmen ! '

There must be something in him. Such great
names imply greatness. Who hath seen Michael
Angelo's things—of us that never pilgrimaged to
Rome — and yet which of us disbelieves his
greatness? How I will revel in his cobwebs and
subtleties, till my brain spins ! "

Of all of which one may only say, that
the man who climbs Parnassus in this
spirit will assuredly have had his reward
in the climbing, even though fatigue bring
death at the top.

The other special field in which the
letters show his critical faculty at work is
the poetry of Coleridge and Wordsworth.
It is not wonderful that he appreciated it,
for they were his friends: where he shows
his strength is in the manner of his appreciation. His weakness, too, perhaps: for
what was highest in his two friends grew
less and less within his reach as the years
went by. He could be enthusiastic as a very
young man over Coleridge's " Religious

Musings," but I very much doubt if he
would have had the same feeling late in
life. It was not only that his life and
habits in middle age were not quite in
tune with these sublimer aspirations. The
fact is, that his taste in poetry was all for
its action and emotion, not at all for its
thought. Of Wordsworth's great poetic
doctrine he shows no sign of knowing
anything. These high matters were in
fact out of his ken: he did not care for
"Faust," nor for the "Hymn to Intellectual
Beauty," nor would he, we may be sure,
have cared for the "In Memoriam," or
"Christmas Eve and Easter Day." But
how admirably he understands and praises
that which did come home to him. I
have quoted what he says of the famous
stanza from "Yarrow Visited." His recognition of the "Ancient Mariner" is as
instantaneous. Southey had written a
cool review of the "Lyrical Ballads."
Lamb puts him right at once.

> "I never so deeply felt the pathetic as in that part—
>> 'A spring of love gush'd from my heart,
>> And I bless'd them unaware.'
> It stung me into high pleasure through sufferings."

He writes also to Wordsworth—

> "I was never so affected with any human tale.
> After first reading it, I was totally possessed with

it for many days. I dislike all the miraculous part of it; but the feelings of the man under the operation of such scenery, dragged me along like Tom Pipe's magic whistle. I totally differ from your idea that the *Marinere* should have had a character and profession. This is a beauty in '*Gulliver's Travels*,' where the mind is kept in a placid state of little wonderments; but the '*Ancient Marinere*' undergoes such trials as overwhelm and bury all individuality or memory of what he was—like the state of a man in a bad dream, one terrible peculiarity of which is, that all consciousness of personality is gone."

It is a hundred years since the " Ancient Mariner " was written ; but has there yet been a critic who has said anything better than this about it ?

Wordsworth's " Tintern Abbey " was naturally less in his way : yet no Wordsworthian can complain of his treatment of it. " The '*Ancient Marinere*' plays more tricks with the mind than that last poem, which is yet one of the finest written." When we remember that the courage to praise was in those days the rarest quality among critics, this prompt and generous tribute must be admitted to do Lamb double honour. When the second volume of "Lyrical Ballads" appeared, he got into trouble with Wordsworth and Coleridge for his inadequate appreciation ; but to us it is more remarkable that he at once singled out for special honour the exquisite lines, " She dwelt among the untrodden ways." In the same letter he lays his finger on the danger to which Wordsworth was all his life exposed. The new volume "too artfully aims," he says, "at simplicity of expression. And you sometimes doubt if Simplicity be not a cover for Poverty." Yet when " The Excursion " comes, he receives it with fine and characteristically phrased enthusiasm. Its poet, he says, " walks through common forests as through some Dodona or enchanted wood, and every casual bird that flits upon the boughs, like that miraculous one in Tasso, but in language more piercing than any articulate sounds, reveals to him far higher love-lays."

But perhaps Lamb is at his best when he is talking of the general principles of all art. With what good sense he protests to Southey :—

"I think you are too apt to conclude faintly, with some cold moral, as in the end of the poem called ' The Victory '—

' Be thou her comforter, who art the widow's friend';

a single common-place line of comfort which bears no relation in weight or number to the many lines which describe suffering. This is to convert religion into mediocre feelings, which should burn, and glow, and tremble. A moral should be wrought into the body and soul, the matter and tendency of a poem, not tagged to the end, like a 'God send the good ship into harbour,' at the conclusion of our bills of lading."

There will probably never be a day when it will be unnecessary for lovers of poetry to repeat this. Those who do not understand what poetry is are always asking her to do work which is not hers. The poet's business is not instruction, but inspiration: not direction, but suggestion. He has no commandments to deliver; only when we go up to commune with him, and look down for once from the heights where he habitually lives, we see all the lowness of low things as we have never seen it before. It is as Goethe said to Eckermann: "if a poet have as high a soul as Sophocles, his influence will always be moral, let him do what he will."

I must allow myself to give one or two more of the excellent pieces of general criticism with which Lamb's letters abound. Here is the passage which contains the phrase quoted above in another connection. He is writing to Wordsworth: it is the letter that produced the " castigation " by return of post from Wordsworth and Coleridge :—

" I will just add that it appears to me a fault in the ' Beggar,' that the instructions conveyed in it are too direct, and like a lecture; they don't slide into the mind of the reader while he is imagining no such matter. An intelligent reader finds a sort of insult in being told, ' I will teach you how to think upon this subject.' This fault, if I am right, is in a ten-thousandth worse degree to be found in Sterne, and in many novelists and modern poets, who continually put a sign-post up to show where you are to feel. They set out with assuming their readers to be stupid ; very different from '*Robinson Crusoe*,' the '*Vicar of Wakefield*,' '*Roderick Random*,' and other beautiful, bare narratives. . . . I am sorry that Coleridge has christened his '*Ancient Marinere*' a *Poet's Reverie :* it is as bad as Bottom the Weaver's declaration, that he is not a lion, but only the scenical representation of a lion. What new idea is gained by this title but one subversive of all credit—which the tale should force upon us—of its truth ! "

The point is not as clearly put as it might be ; but what he felt with true critical sense is the thing which is perhaps of all things about art the most frequently overlooked. The business of art is to suggest, not to say. Something must be left to the imagination. Why is it that to the man who is sensitive to the impressions of art, sketches are so often far more attractive than finished pictures ! Why does black and white so often beat colour ? It is because art makes its appeal in part to the sense of wonder, and the imagination dislikes an imitation that too closely resembles the fact, preferring to have something of the strange and incomplete and unknown to range in. That is why, for instance, illustrations to poetry are, as Lamb knew, nearly always detestable. "To be tied down," as he complains, "to an authentic face of Juliet! to have Imogen's portrait; to confine the illimitable!" In the same way the landscape which suggests no field of space beyond itself is a failure, and the picture of any sort which tells all its tale, and never manages to send us dreaming outside it, is as bad as the fairy tale which begins by explaining itself to be an allegory. The law in poetry is just the same, and one of the reasons why French poetry fails by the side of our own, is that the French poet is apt to express and explain himself till the mystery is gone, and with it the charm, the grace, in fact, the poetry.

Lamb knew that this was a fundamental law of art, to be applied everywhere. He applies it admirably to John Martin's painting "Belshazzar," where he complains with reference to the writing on the wall " the *type* is as plain as Baskerville's: they should have been dim, full of mystery, letters to the mind rather than the eye." He goes on to illustrate from the same picture another central principle of art and literature, especially his favourite dramatic literature, the law of unity of interest.

" Rembrandt has painted only Belshazzar and a courtier or two (taking a part of the banquet for

the whole), not fribbled out a mob of fine folks.
Then everything is (*i.e.,* in Martin's picture) so
distinct, to the very necklaces, and that foolish
little prophet. What *one* point is there of interest ?
The ideal of such a subject is that you, the spec-
tator, should see nothing but what at the time you
would have seen—the *hand*, and the *King*—not
to be at leisure to make tailor-remarks on the
dresses, or, Dr. Kitchener-like, to examine the
good things at table. Just such a confused piece
is his ' Joshua,' frittered into a thousand fragments,
little armies here, little armies there—you should
see only the *Sun* and *Joshua.*"

There is not a gallery in Europe which
does not show how much the constant
reiteration of this criticism is needed ; nor
have we to go beyond the bounds of the
greatest of dramatists to see the difference
—in " Othello," for instance, and " Antony
and Cleopatra "—between a play which has
one action and a few characters seen only in
relation to it, and another where the super-
abundance of actors obscures the action
and makes the list of *dramatis personæ*
as necessary as a dictionary to a man
struggling with a foreign language.

Once more hear Lamb on a question
even more vital to our day than to his :

" ' Goody Two Shoes ' is almost out of print.
Mrs. Barbauld's stuff has banished all the old
classics of the nursery ; and the shopman at New-
berry's hardly deigned to reach them off an old

exploded corner of a shelf, when Mary asked for them. . . . Knowledge insignificant and vapid as Mrs. Barbauld's books convey, it seems, must come to a child in the *shape of knowledge;* and his empty noddle must be turned with conceit of his own powers when he has learnt that a horse is an animal, and Billy is better than a horse, and such like, instead of that beautiful interest in wild tales, which made the child a man, while all the time he suspected himself to be no bigger than a child. Science has succeeded to poetry no less in the little walks of children than with men. Is there no possibility of averting this sore evil ? "

This is no place for discussing one of the largest of modern questions, which, by the way, receives its ablest treatment, perhaps, in Matthew Arnold's admirable lecture on Literature and Science, reprinted in his " Discourses in America "; but those who to-day see the " sore evil " of science, so excellent in its own field, ruining art and literature by the ignorant demand for more and ever more fact, realism, literalism, and therefore less and less imagination, creative power, life, are bound to give Lamb due credit for his foresight. And they will share with him and Arnold the conviction that physical science, which deals with matter, can never have the same educational value as literature, which deals with spirit.

But it is time to leave the literary critic

and give a few specimens of the man as he would have been if he had never written a page ; his humour, his affections, his weaknesses, his simple pleasures. He lived the quietest, most monotonous life. It is true that it falls to the lot of very few men to have so awful an experience as that one terrible tragedy in his ; but, for the rest, few men have had so even an existence. The office all day, tea at six, supper at nine, was for him an unbroken routine. The subjects of his letters, apart from books, are his little meetings with his friends, the small doings of his sister and himself, perpetual lamentations that they could not be greater because the " Den in Leadenhall" kept him so close imprisoned.

"This dead, everlasting dead desk,—how it weighs the spirit of a gentleman down!" . . . "I wish I were a Caravan driver, or a Penny postman, to earn my bread in air and sunshine." . . . "Oh! that I had been a shoemaker, or a baker, or a man of large, independent fortune! Oh, darling laziness! Heaven of Epicurus! Saint's Everlasting Rest! that I could drink vast potations of thee thro' unmeasured Eternity—Otium *cum*, vel *sine* dignitate. Scandalous, dishonourable—any kind of *repose*. I stand not upon the dignified sort. Accursed, damned desks, trade, commerce, business! Inventions of the old original busy-body, brain-working Satan — Sabbathless, restless Satan ! A curse relieves; do you ever try it ?"

"A strange letter to write to a lady," as he himself justly says ; but for us now the feelings of the lady, which it necessarily leaves unknown, are of less consequence than those of Lamb, which it reveals. They were constant, at any rate on the surface, and grew stronger than ever when the Company abolished the old saint's-day holidays which had been customary. But he can play prettily with his grievances as with everything else.

"I have but one holiday, which is Christmas Day itself nakedly; no pretty garnish and fringes of St. John's Day, Holy Innocents, etc., that used to bestud it all around in the calendar. *Improbe labor !* I write six hours every day in this candle-light fog-den at Leadenhall."

Yet when Bernard Barton thought of giving up his bank clerkship for literature, the advice of the oldest, coldest, and wisest of family solicitors, though it might have been duller than Lamb's, could not possibly have been more prudent. It is an admirable letter.

"'Throw yourself on the world without any rational plan of support, beyond what the chance employ of booksellers would afford you ! ! ! '
"Throw yourself rather, my dear sir, from the steep Tarpeian rock, slap-dash headlong upon iron spikes. If you had but five consolatory minutes between the desk and the bed, make much of them,

and live a century in them, rather than turn slave, to the booksellers. They are Turks and Tartars when they have poor authors at their beck. Hitherto you have been at arm's length from them. Come not within their grasp. I have known many authors for bread, some repining, others envying the blessed security of a counting-house, all agreeing they would rather have been tailors, weavers, —what not, rather than the thing they were. I have known some starved, some to go mad, one dear friend literally dying in a workhouse. You know not what a rapacious, dishonest set these booksellers are. Ask even Southey, who (a single case almost) has made a fortune by book drudgery, what he has found them. Oh, you know not (may you never know!) the miseries of subsisting by authorship. 'Tis a pretty appendage to a situation like yours or mine; but a slavery worse than all slavery, to be a bookseller's dependant, to drudge your brains for pots of ale and breasts of mutton, to change your free thoughts and voluntary numbers for ungracious task-work. . . . Keep to your bank, and the bank will keep you. . . . I bless every star that Providence, not seeing good to make me independent, has seen it next good to settle me upon the stable foundation of Leadenhall. Sit down, good B. B., in the banking office. What! Is there not from six to eleven p.m. six days in the week, and is there not all Sunday? Fie, what a superfluity of man's time, if you could but think so!— enough for relaxation, mirth, converse, poetry, good thoughts, quiet thoughts. . . . Henceforth I retract all my fond complaints of mercantile employment; look upon them but as lovers' quarrels."

Where will you find a letter in which common sense, poetry, and humour are more delightfully united ? This, and not the man of puns and oddities, is the true Lamb, the Lamb that will live. Hear another letter to the same Barton where the humour plays more freely, but the common sense is just as plain. Barton was nervous about his health. Lamb replies :

" The best way in these cases is to keep yourself as ignorant as you can, as ignorant as the world was before Galen, of the entire inner construction of the animal man ; not to be conscious of a midriff ; to hold kidneys (save of sheep and swine) to be an agreeable fiction ; not to know whereabout the gall grows ; to account the circulation of the blood an idle whimsey of Harvey's ; to acknowledge no mechanism not visible. For, once fix the seat of your disorder, and your fancies flux into it like bad humours. . . . Above all, use exercise, take a little more spirituous liquors, learn to smoke, continue to keep a good conscience, and avoid tampering with hard terms of art—viscosity, scirrhosity, and those bugbears by which simple patients are scared into their graves. Believe the general sense of the mercantile world, which holds that desks are not deadly. .It is the mind, good B. B., and not the limbs, that taints by long sitting. Think of the patience of tailors ! Think how long the Lord Chancellor sits ! Think of the brooding hen ! "

Such a letter is worth many doctors' prescriptions. Yet Lamb, like wiser men, could preach better than he could practise. The demonstrated utility of Leadenhall Street was often less visible to him than its felt disagreeableness. There is, indeed, one part of his advice to Barton which he followed only too well. "Take a little more spirituous liquors; learn to smoke." His letters are full of resolutions:

"I am afraid I must leave off drinking." "I am a poor creature, but I am leaving off gin." "I am the same as when you knew me, almost to a surfeiting identity. This very night I am going to *leave off tobacco!*" "I have positive hopes that I shall be able to conquer smoking!" "I am sensible of the want of method in this letter, but I have been deprived of the connecting organ by a practice I have fallen into since I left Paris, of taking too much strong spirits at night." "I am ill at present; an illness of my own procuring last night: who is perfect?"

Who is perfect? Not poor Lamb, certainly. It is the same story from the day he bitterly reproached himself for "wasting and teasing" his sister's life "for five years past incessantly with my cursed drinking habits and ways of going on," till the day when he visits his adopted daughter, and she is obliged, "the first moment we were alone," to take him into a corner with "Now, pray, don't *drink;* do check yourself after dinner, for my sake." His is no perfect character, in this or in some other ways. There is a curious heartlessness, for instance, in his nature, or, at least, some strange affectation of it, which lets him recount the saddest stories without a trace of sympathy. His friend is ruined, and he reflects jokingly on the prudent conduct which has kept for him and his a warm fire and a snug roof over their heads. A servant girl is inconvenient enough to be ill in his lodgings: "If she died, it were something: gladly would I pay the coffin-maker." Princess Charlotte dies amid universal grief, felt as grief for royal deaths rarely is felt, and Lamb comments: "What a nice holyday I got on Wednesday by favour of a princess dying!" Yet it is probably fairer, as well as pleasanter, to explain this curious attitude as a piece of his whimsical turn for being unlike other people. No one was ever more active in trying to help his broken-down acquaintances, even, for instance, the very one whose ruin he records so complacently. No one loved the few he did love more unreservedly than he. Hear him telling Crabb Robinson about his old friend Randal Norris, sub-treasurer of the Inner Temple:

" In him I have a loss the world cannot make up. He was my friend, and my father's friend, all the life I can remember. I seem to have made foolish friendships ever since. Those are friendships which outlive a second generation. Old as I am waxing, in his eyes I was still the child he first knew me. To the last he called me Charley. I

have none to call me Charley now. He was the
last link that bound me to the Temple. You
are but of yesterday. In him seem to have
died the old plainness of manners and single-
ness of heart. Letters he knew nothing of, nor
did his reading extend beyond the pages of the
Gentleman's Magazine. Yet there was a pride of
literature about him from being amongst books (he
was librarian), and from some scraps of doubtful
Latin which he had picked up in his office of
entering students, that gave him very diverting
airs of pedantry. Can I forget the erudite look
with which, when he had been in vain trying to
make out a black-letter text of Chaucer in the
Temple Library, he laid it down and told me that—
' In those old books, Charley, there is sometimes a
deal of very indifferent spelling'; and seemed to
console himself in the reflection ! His jokes, for he
had his jokes, are now ended ; but they were old
trusty perennials, staples that pleased after *decies
repetita*, and were always as good as new. One
song he had, which was reserved for the night of
Christmas Day, which we always spent in the
Temple. It was an old thing, and spoke of the
flat bottoms of our foes, and the possibility of their
coming over in darkness, and alluded to threats of
an invasion many years blown over ; and when
he came to the part—

" ' We'll still make 'em run, and we'll still make 'em sweat,
In spite of the Devil and *Brussels Gazette*,'

his eyes would sparkle as with the freshness of an
impending event. And what is the *Brussels Gazette*
now ? I cry while I enumerate these trifles, ' How
shall we tell them in a stranger's ear ? ' "

And then he sets to thinking of what

can be done for his old friend's family.
It is not only of FitzGerald that one may
say, "his friendships were like loves."

Into his most sacred relation of all, his
love for his sister, I have little inclination
to intrude.   Literature   knows   of   no
brother and sister who have stood in so
beautiful a relation.   They took each
other, as he says, "for better, for worse":
and never was truer or purer affection.

"To say all that I know of her would be more
than I think anybody could believe, or even understand; and when I hope to have her well again
with me, it would be sinning against her feelings to
go about to praise her; for I can conceal nothing
that I do from her. She is older, and wiser, and
better than I, and all my wretched imperfections I
cover to myself by resolutely thinking on her goodness. She would share life and death, heaven and
hell, with me."

They had not lived together long when
this was written; he had then nearly
thirty years longer to be with her. With
her he lived while at work and with her
he went on his yearly holiday. To his
unselfish affection there seemed "something of dishonesty" in pleasures taken
without her. And so it remained to the
end. No shadow of change ever came
upon their love from the day when one of
her earlier illnesses drew from him the

beautiful letter, part of which I have quoted, to that in which he wrote to Wordsworth—during the last eclipse of her reason, or last but one, which he lived to see—

"I see little of her; alas! I too often hear her. *Sunt lachrymae rerum!* and you and I must bear it."

A year and a half after these words were written, the long partnership was over, and Landor addressed his beautiful consolation to the sister who was to live thirteen sad years more.

" Comfort thee, O thou mourner, yet awhile !
    Again shall Elia's smile
Refresh thy heart, where heart can ache no more.
    What is it we deplore ?

" He leaves behind him, freed from griefs and years,
    Far worthier things than tears.
The love of friends without a single foe :
    Unequalled lot below !

" His gentle soul, his genius, these are thine ;
    For these dost thou repine ?
He may have left the lowly walks of men ;
    Left them he has ; what then ?

" Are not his footsteps followed by the eyes
    Of all the good and wise ?
Tho' the warm day is over, yet they seek
    Upon the lofty peak

" Of his pure mind the roseate light that glows
    O'er death's perennial snows.
Behold him ! from the region of the blest
    He speaks ; he bids thee rest."

EDWARD FITZGERALD.[1]

WHEN Edward FitzGerald died in June, 1883, only a few people had even heard his name. Indeed the public at large had not had much chance of hearing it. He had published very little; and the private, or semi-private, method of publication he adopted, his retiring temper, which led him, as some one said, to take "more pains to avoid fame than others do to seek it," the subjects his works dealt with, remote from most men's reading, and appealing only to the finer and more curious part of the small public which reads—all alike combined to keep him quite unknown. Nor could the dedication of Tennyson's "Tiresias," written just before FitzGerald died, but, as the Epilogue

[1] First printed in the "Quarterly Review," July, 1896. FitzGerald's Letters are to be found in the following volumes: 1. "Letters and Literary Remains of Edward FitzGerald." Edited by William Aldis Wright. Three volumes. London, 1889. 2. "Letters of Edward FitzGerald." Edited by William Aldis Wright. Two volumes. London, 1894. 3. "Letters of Edward FitzGerald to Fanny Kemble." Edited by William Aldis Wright. London, 1895.

shows, not published till after his death, do much to dissipate this obscurity. In spite of all its cordial friendliness,—in spite of its generous praise of his

> " golden Eastern lay,
> Than which I know no version done
> In English more divinely well ; "—

the tribute scarcely widened the circle of those who knew FitzGerald. The memory of many disappointments is apt to keep the judicious reader from meddling with translations of great poems, and Persian literature is to most men a new field, into which they are shy to break. Tennyson's lines, moreover, because of their enthusiasm, created a suspicion of the partiality of old friendship, and, above all, "Omar Khayyam" was anything but easy to obtain.

So it was that FitzGerald died almost unknown. And yet he was not only a personality, which is a thing rarer than ever now, when everybody lives in the streets and reads the newspapers, but even a very delightful personality. He went his own way from the beginning and lived his own life, and the result was an original creation, such as we look rather to find in the great novelists than in actual life. No figure could stand out more curiously in our modern English world. Nothing is more old-fashioned nowadays than leisure, and FitzGerald was at leisure all his days. Nor could anything be more old-fashioned than his use of it. His taste was all for old books and old friends, familiar jokes and familiar places. He clung all his life to the plain Suffolk country in which he was born ("one of the ugliest places in England, and one of the dullest," he once called it with a good deal less than justice), in the same way as, at the end of his life, he returned every year, with the return of the spring, to his dearly loved Madame de Sévigné. The altars of our great modern idols, bustle and publicity, received no sacrifices from him. Perfectly regardless of time and money and fashion, he stalked his native roads in a strange costume—in which, however, it is said, he never ceased to have an indefinable look of the *hidalgo* about him—or pottered in his boat on the sluggish Deben, asking children odd questions, or looking over Crabbe or Calderon. He had a just horror of clever people, and much preferred the stupidity of country folks to the "impudence of Londoners." His time was largely passed with his social inferiors; with the boys who read to him when his eyes began to fail, and who must have been bewildered by his strange sayings and doings; with the bookseller who valued his friendship then and still affectionately cherishes his memory; or with the "hero" fisherman of Lowestoft who, "great man" as he was, had a weakness which he could not conquer, and proved, as far as money went, one of FitzGerald's bad speculations. Not that that would have troubled FitzGerald: his generosity was, like everything else about him, of the old-fashioned sort, which, though certainly not the best or wisest, is at least the prettiest: free and open, careless of distant results, and very direct and personal in its application. I imagine it to be very possible that he never gave a guinea to a charitable society in his life, but very certain that he gave a great many to unfortunate individuals with whom he came in contact.

Altogether it was a strange existence, with something about it that may well make us pause in our fussy self-importance. Carlyle saw in it all only a "peaceable, affectionate, ultra-modest man," and an "innocent *far niente* life"; but, after all, for a man to have made himself "peaceable, affectionate, and ultra-modest," is to have done something, and something which to his neighbours is of far more value than many more shining performances. Perhaps, too, we are apt nowadays to undervalue the higher sort of innocency, and to forget that there is old authority for the doctrine that it is just innocence which "brings a man peace at the last," and that another authority, still higher if not quite so old, makes "pure religion" itself consist in two things, one of which is keeping oneself "unspotted from the world." Besides, from a humbler point of view, or indeed from any point of view whatever, manliness and cheerfulness, generosity and gentleness and pure unadulterated simplicity, must always be things worth having. Even if "the world's coarse thumb" asks as usual for results more material and tangible, the attainment of such graces will always redeem a life like FitzGerald's from the charge of having been wasted and useless. Any such charge is, however, absurd enough, apart from these considerations; for the translator of Omar Khayyam is assuredly not without his "proper reason for existing."

A life like FitzGerald's has no story. He was born at Bredfield, near Woodbridge, in 1809. The chief recollection he seems to have retained of his childhood was the rather terrible if very splendid

figure of his mother, a great lady who used
to astonish the neighbourhood with her
coach and four, and who seems to have had
a great lady's temper. He went to school
at Bury St. Edmund's, where he began
his long friendships with William Donne,
who was afterwards Censor of Plays,
and with Spedding, the editor of Bacon.
It was at Cambridge that he made the
acquaintance of Thackeray, who spoke
affectionately of him on his deathbed,
and of Thompson, afterwards Master of
Trinity, FitzGerald's college. He followed
no profession after taking his degree.
Till 1853, though he often shifted his
quarters, he lived mainly in a thatched
cottage at Boulge, near Woodbridge, just
outside the gate of his brother's place,
Boulge Hall. He was in lodgings in
Woodbridge from 1860 to 1874, when he
settled in a small house of his own outside
the town, named, by command of some
lady who visited him, Little Grange. And
" Laird of Little Grange," as he liked to
sign himself, he remained till he died, quite
suddenly, in June, 1883. He is buried
in Boulge churchyard; and a rose, the
daughter of one that grows on Omar
Khayyam's tomb, has been planted over
his grave. The text on the stone, " It is

He that hath made us, and not we ourselves," was his own choice.

The little he wrote was all published
anonymously, except "Six Dramas of
Calderon," in 1853. He prefixed a
memoir to an edition of the poems of
his friend Bernard Barton, the Quaker
poet of Woodbridge, in 1849. Two years
later, he printed his remarkable dialogue
"Euphranor." "Polonius" appeared in
1852; a rendering of the "Agamemnon,"
parts of which are unequalled, was published in 1876; and four editions of his
translation of "Omar Khayyam" came
out before his death, the first appearing
in 1859, without gaining any immediate
recognition. The other Persian translations were left in manuscript and only
appeared in Mr. Aldis Wright's edition of
his "Literary Remains," 1889.

He was a man of many and notable
friendships, chiefly kept up by interchange
of letters. Those friendships that date
from Bury and Cambridge have been given;
others that followed, to be extinguished only
by death, united him to Alfred Tennyson
and Frederick Tennyson, Carlyle, and
Carlyle's friend and editor, Norton; to
Barton the poet, and Lawrence the
painter; to Sir Frederick Pollock, Lowell,

two Crabbes, son and grandson of his favourite poet; to Archbishop Trench, Professor Cowell, who led him to read Persian, and Mr. Aldis Wright, whom he appointed his literary executor.

It used to be said that a man is known by his friends. If that be so, the world which knows his friends so well has no need of an introduction to FitzGerald. The companion of men like these was certainly no ordinary man, either in heart or head. Nor would it be possible to keep on writing dull letters to such men for forty years. FitzGerald's letters then, we know beforehand, are not dull. In fact they are among the best in the language, and it is possible that they may find not many less readers than "Omar Khayyam"; though, no doubt, but for " Omar Khayyam," we should never have heard of them. Letters show the man, and we have Fitz-Gerald here set out before us, just as he was, in all his kindliness and humour, in all his fine and acute perception of true and false in art and literature, in his love of all that is truly lovable, in his queer ways and whims, even in his weaknesses. A man with his tastes could not write to such men as those to whom his letters went, without often talking of things,

books and pictures and music, for instance, that are not likely to be soon forgotten ; and of things, too, whose interest
is everlasting, the spring and the birds
and the sea. On such subjects as these,
his letters are full of good sayings, sayings
with the personal mark upon them, fresh
and worth the utterance, if often in substance very old. Indeed, there is something one would like to quote on almost
every page ; and it would not be hard to
make a large volume of extracts from
them, on the Book of Beauties principle,
which, detestable as it assuredly would
be as a book, would yet contain nothing
unworthy of insertion.

Hundreds of new books appear every
week, and it is for the reviewer to warn
the public against those which are not
worth reading, and to introduce to the
public those which are. But he has a
third duty, certainly not less important, to
do with regard to old books, one which
has been the special delight of all the
great critics. He has to call the public
back, from time to time, to old friends
whom it might otherwise forget. The
first duty or the second has been often
only a pleasant excuse for the third.
Sainte-Beuve will write on a new edition

of Molière or La Fontaine, and Matthew Arnold will review a new translation of Marcus Aurelius, not because they want to praise or blame the new edition, but because they want, and want very much, to fetch down Molière and Marcus Aurelius from that upper shelf on which forgetful or ungrateful people are too apt to leave them. So, in this case of Edward FitzGerald, there is a little of two duties to do. Nothing assuredly of the first I spoke of, the business of warning; but something of the second, for there is a new volume of FitzGerald's Letters, those to Fanny Kemble, just reprinted from "Temple Bar"; and, as to the third duty, there are the old letters and the old friends, whom the public has known, or ought to have known long ago, to recall to all our memories again.

There are a dozen ways in which this might be done. However, in FitzGerald's case, it is not what he did or wrote that we want so much to remember, but what he was. It is as a personality even more than as a poet that we think of him. When we are calling an old friend to mind, the best way of bringing him before us again as he was, is to think of the things he cared most about. So there will be no better way of getting at the

living picture of FitzGerald than by
hearing him talk of some of the things
that gave him most pleasure.

And first, of music. There was nothing
he cared for more. His taste in it was,
like all his tastes, a little old-fashioned,
for he preferred melody to harmony and
Italian music to German. He was himself always fond of singing, from the
Cambridge days when Thackeray and he
sang together, to those later on when he
would " trudge through the mud " of an
evening to Bredfield Vicarage and go
through one of Handel's Coronation
Anthems with Crabbe, his poet's son.

" With not a voice among us," as he says;
" laughable it may seem, yet it is not quite so; the
things are so well-defined, simple, and grand, that
the faintest outline of them tells; my admiration of
the old Giant grows and grows; his is the Music
for a Great, Active, People. . . .

" Sometimes, too, I go over to a place elegantly
called *Bungay*, where a Printer lives who drills the
young folks of a manufactory there to sing in
Chorus once a week. . . . They sing some of the
English Madrigals, some of Purcell, and some of
Handel, in a way to satisfy me, who believe that
the *grandest* things do not depend on delicate
finish. If you were here now, we would go over
and hear the Harmonious Blacksmith sung in
Chorus, with words, of course. It almost made me
cry when I heard the divine Air rolled into vocal
harmony from the four corners of a large Hall."

That was the music he loved, and could keep up in the country, the old English music and Handel; but he did not stop there. Indeed he preferred Mozart to Handel, who, he says, "never gets out of his wig." He admired Beethoven : "the finale of C minor is very noble," but " Beethoven is gloomy " ; and, as he said of poetry, FitzGerald admitted nothing into his Paradise " but such as breathe content, and virtue." He detested Wagner, and in Bizet's " Carmen " he saw nothing but "very beautiful accompaniments to no melody," which, after all, is more than many quite sane people saw in it at first. He thought indeed that in French music as in "all French things " there was an absence of the " Holy of Holies far withdrawn." Beethoven, on the other hand, he quite felt was "original, majestic, and profound," with " a depth not to be reached all at once." But perhaps he was,

"strictly speaking, more of a thinker than a musician. A great genius he was somehow. . . . He tried to think in music; almost to reason in music; whereas, perhaps, we should be contented with *feeling* in it. It can never speak very definitely. There is that famous ' Holy, Holy, Lord God Almighty,' &c., in Handel; nothing can sound more simple and devotional; but it is only lately adapted to these

words, being originally (I believe) a love-song in
'Rodelinda.'   Then the famous music of 'He
layeth the beams of his chambers in the waters,'
&c., was originally fitted to an Italian pastoral song
—'Nasce al bosco in rozza cuna, un felice pastorello,'
&c.   That part which seems so well to describe
'and walketh on the wings of the wind' falls
happily in with 'e con l'aura di fortuna' with
which this pastorello sailed along.   The character
of the music is ease and largeness ; as the shepherd
lived, so God Almighty walked on the wind. . . .
Music is so far the most universal language, that
any one piece in a particular strain symbolizes all
the analogous phenomena, spiritual or material—if
you can talk of spiritual phenomena."

Therefore "it can never speak very
definitely" ; and, in part at least for that
reason, Mozart is "incontestably the
purest *musician;* Beethoven would have
been Poet or Painter as well."   He
believed as much in Mozart's power as
in his beauty.

"People cannot believe that Mozart is *powerful,*
because he is so Beautiful ; in the same way as it
requires a very practised eye (more than I possess)
to recognize the consummate power predominating
in the tranquil Beauty of Greek sculpture."

Perhaps this is not all true, and certainly
it is not all new ; but every one will admit
that FitzGerald's firmness and terseness
are qualities not invariably found in
musical criticism.

But music, after all, gives us only a

side-light on FitzGerald's character. It is what he says about books that must supply the central light of the picture. He may be said to have spent his life in enjoying nature and friendship and good books. As friends died or grew too old to visit or be visited, and as nature, with increasing age, came more and more to mean his strip of garden "quarter-deck," books became during the last years of his life almost his sole companions. Fifty years spent in their society naturally made him a very good judge of them. He had his limitations, of course. Probably no one was ever quite catholic enough to enjoy everything that is good in all sorts and conditions of literature. And the note of catholicity is nowhere less to be looked for than in an eccentric recluse with a strongly-marked personality like Fitz-Gerald. His tastes were his own, and he would not always try to give a reason for them, preferring sometimes in these matters, as he said, "*Fell-osophy*" to philosophy. But if his likes and dislikes were ever unreasonable, they were not in the least capricious. His preference was for books of a particular class, quite definite enough to be marked off from others without much difficulty. The key-note to his taste is struck in the words I have already quoted from an early letter, when he says of a collection of poems he was making, "I admit nothing into my Paradise but such as breathe content, and virtue"; that is the negative side of the definition of literature as he laid it down. He could not tolerate the " problem " literature, with which the last two generations have been deluged. The novel or play which has for its backbone a discussion of the religious question, or the marriage question, or the social question, would, of course, have been more than intolerable to him. Literature in fact for him, although he would not have put it in that way, was a fine art, and could have no end beyond itself. He not only abhorred all books with a purpose, but the whole literature of " storm and stress," all striving and crying in the literary market-place. He never succeeded in reading George Eliot, nor did repeated efforts carry him through any of the translations of " Faust." We may agree or disagree, but his position is at any rate clear enough. He could not open his eyes in an atmosphere of confusion or negation, and therefore he never saw the things that are really great in " Faust." And the things that most interested George Eliot were simply tiresome to FitzGerald. He asked of his favourites ease, serenity, lightness of touch, some indulgence for human follies and frailties, simplicity and directness, a store of humour to light up the way and a large humanity to smooth it. *Non omnes omnia,* of course, but authors so entirely without many of these qualities as Goethe and George Eliot, or again Browning, could never be among his friends. The serene and wise old man of Eckermann's "Conversations," "almost as repeatedly to be read as Boswell's ' Johnson,' " he did indeed know and like, and he must, it may be thought, have appreciated the poet of the shorter poems if he had known them; but the troubled and self-conscious author of "Faust" or "Wilhelm Meister" did not appeal to him. Goethe is in fact inclined to pose a little, as George Eliot is a little inclined to preach, and neither habit was much to FitzGerald's taste.

His special favourites, then, were Cervantes and Scott, and Madame de Sévigné and Montaigne; that old delightful humour, in fact, which only overlaid a ground of seriousness always present underneath. For that is the real difference between the old humour, which felt so deeply for our *pauvre et triste humanité,* and the new, which only sneers at it with bitter heartlessness, or sits down with pleasure to the spectacle of its calamities. To FitzGerald's friends and favourites, life, whatever else it was, was always a thing of infinite meaning. Nor did he always ask that it should be seen with the eye of humour. To " see it steadily and see it whole," as Sophocles and Shakespeare did, was in itself a sure passport to his love ; and to see it as Dante or Æschylus saw it, blazing in the light cast by a grand and daring imagination, and yet deal with it under the restrictions of consummate art, secured at once his enthusiastic admiration. He was not afraid indeed of the old problems provided they were treated in the old way, the Æschylean way of awe and reverence, the Sophoclean way of quietness and confidence, Dante's way of assured serenity of faith. These high matters, he would no doubt have said, were not things to talk much about, certainly not to be contentious or querulous about; the fit place for them is not the tongue, not even perhaps altogether the head, but something deeper down, the mysterious recesses of the heart, where they find such solution as may be, or, what is sometimes best of all, no other solution but that of silence.

This was what he cared about, then : literature in the sense which is at once the plainest and the highest ; the thing in itself; not bricks and straw for building moral or political edifices, but the very picture of our common humanity, a food on which men can live, raised on the good soil of life itself. Politics he hated : " Don't write politics," he says to Frederick Tennyson ; " I agree with you beforehand." Even for history he cared very little ; " never having read any History but Herodotus, I believe "; though the statement is not literally true, for we find him reading Thucydides and Tacitus. History, for his taste, dealt too much with politics, that is, with the comparatively transient and external, and dwelt too little on the permanent things in our nature, which lie below untouched by any change, and remain substantially the same in all ages and countries. The one exception that he made is readily understood. He liked Herodotus for his presentment of man face to face with the unchanging destinies, his study of old ways and old tales, and the humour which he may not have meant, but which we cannot help finding in him.

But let us hear him talk of some of his favourites. And first of novelists : from

Boccaccio, by whose help, as he tells Mrs. Kemble in October, 1876, he "makes a kind of Summer in his Room" at Lowestoft, to Dickens, whom, in spite of faults, he "must look on as a mighty Benefactor to Mankind"; "a little Shakespeare—a Cockney Shakespeare, if you will; but as distinct, if not so great, a piece of pure Genius as was born in Stratford." He even wished to "go and worship at Gadshill, as I have worshipped at Abbotsford, though with less Reverence, to be sure." There are very few in the long line of whom he has not something to say. He never tired of "Don Quixote," which he thought "the most delightful of all books": "I have had Don Quixote, Boccaccio, and my dear Sophocles (once more) for company on board: the first of these so delightful, that I got to love the very Dictionary in which I had to look out the words." "Gil Blas" he could not read; no doubt because of the formal resemblance to his favourite Don, which forces into painful prominence the contrast between the essential vulgarity of Le Sage's hero and the perfect gentleman created by Cervantes. He preferred Richardson to ·Fielding, and was particularly fond of Clarissa, of which he quotes Tennyson as saying, "I love those large, *still* Books." To Miss Austen he objected that " she never goes out of the Parlour," but admitted that he thought her " quite capital in a Circle I have found quite unendurable to walk in." Trollope is, for him, " not perfect like Miss Austen, but then so much wider scope." Of some other novels of modern day, he well complains that they " are painfully microscopic and elaborate on dismal subjects." Scott alone he thought worthy to stand with Cervantes, and he is justly indignant with Carlyle for wanting to set up " such a cantankerous, narrow-minded Bigot as John Knox," as Scotland's national hero in Sir Walter's stead. No one ever loved Scott more or better than FitzGerald did; the man, if possible, more than the writer. He liked his men of letters to be men of action too, and he was one of those to whom the thought of Scott and Shakespeare, active in business public and private, is only less pleasing than that of Æschylus at Marathon, Cervantes at Lepanto, or Thucydides, ὅς ταῦτα ξυνέγραψεν, at Amphipolis. Scott, in fact, was a man of exactly the type which always won his affections—large and generous, absolutely modest and unpretending, not merely a perfect gentleman, but what he called "A Man." He could even go so far as to compare unfavourably the conscientious workmanship of Tennyson and Thackeray with Scott's curious and surely rather foolish "You know that I don't care a curse about what I write "—a passage over which some of his devoutest worshippers have stumbled; for if a man spends time in writing, surely it is the part of sense and manliness to take care to do it well. However, we will not quarrel with Fitz-Gerald. Our debt of gratitude to Scott is one too large to pay, and to try to pay it by praising his very faults is itself a fault that leans to virtue's side. We can sympathise with his pleasure in quoting Barry Cornwall's fine remark when he saw Scott among other authors at Rogers's: "I do not think any one envied him any more than one envies Kings "; with his "going to worship" at Abbotsford, as to Stratford-on-Avon, and seeing "that it was good to have so done "; and, still more intimately, with his "having the 'Fortunes of Nigel' at night—a little of it, and not every night—for the reason that I do not wish to eat my Cake too soon."

He was very fond, too, of a few in that pleasant company among whom he was himself to take so distinguished a place, and who are, indeed, novelists, too, in their way, filling their galleries with living portraits instead of fictitious; Cowper, whom he knew in Southey's Life, and Walpole, whose letters he puts with Cowper's as the best in the language: " I can scarce imagine better Christmas fare," he says, and " I think I could show you that he had a very loving Heart for a few, and a very firm, just, understanding, under all his Wit and Fun. Even Carlyle has admitted that he was about the clearest-sighted Man of his time." Then there was Mrs. Trench, whom he strangely places after Cowper and Walpole; Lamb, of whose life he made a calendar as a companion to the Letters; and of course, and above all, Madame de Sévigné. He read her for the first time eight years before he died, having before " kept aloof from her, because of that eternal Daughter of hers; but 'it's all Truth and Daylight,' as Kitty Clive said of Mrs. Siddons." The acquaintance once made, he renewed it every spring, made a dictionary of her *dramatis personæ*, and was fond of quoting the advice Sainte Beuve gave one summer

day in the troubles of 1871 : "*Lisons tout
Madame de Sévigné.*"   There is no one of
whom he speaks with more affection.

"*Ho ! parlons d'autres choses, ma fille*, as my dear
Sévigné says.   She now occupies Montaigne's
place in my room ; well—worthily : she herself a
Lover of Montaigne, and with a spice of his free
thought and speech in her.   I am sometimes vext
I never made her acquaintance till last year ; but
perhaps it was as well to have such an acquaintance
reserved for one's latter years.   The fine Creature !
much more alive to me than most Friends—I *should*
like to see her ' Rochers ' in Brittany."

In another place, he lets fall an admirable
bit of criticism : " Half her Beauty is the
liquid melodiousness of her language—all
unpremeditated as a Blackbird's."
All these were intimate friends, to be
enjoyed on a footing of easy equality.
But he spent as much time perhaps in
the society of higher people, with whom
none of us may dare to be familiar, so
that even he, poet as he was, and himself
the frankest of men, not apt to be daunted
by great names, confesses to reading
Milton "with wonder and a sort of awe."
Elsewhere, also, he has a fine saying, too
easily missed from its simplicity : " I take
pleasure in reading things I don't wholly
understand ; just as the old women like
sermons : I think it is of a piece with an

admiration of all Nature around us." The greater poets were constantly in his hands, as may be seen everywhere in his letters; and it is on what he did for them that his fame must chiefly rest. He believed in translations, and wished Tennyson to devote "his diminished powers to translating Sophocles or Æschylus, as I fancy a poet should do—*one* work, at any rate, of his great Predecessors." He thought the many failures were due to want of freedom, and that if translators "would not hamper themselves with Forms of Verse, and Thought, irreconcilable with English Language and English Ways of Thinking," they would succeed very well, and he went far to prove it by his own success. He did not pretend, as he was always modestly saying, to genius but to taste; and his judgment very rarely lost its way. We cannot follow it all the way, perhaps, as to his "eternal Crabbe," whom he is always quoting and rearranging; but early associations, the claims of Suffolk, the ties of friendship with the poet's son and grandson, may well excuse in this respect a little extravagance. He does not deceive himself about Omar, who made his fame: "Oh dear," he writes to Cowell, "when I do look into Homer, Dante and

Virgil, Æschylus, Shakespeare, etc., these Orientals look—silly! Don't resent my saying so. *Don't* they?" And yet he loved Omar, though he will not grant him a place in that company. Here is a picture which is proof enough of his affection:

"When in Bedfordshire, I put away almost all books except Omar Khayyám! which I could not help looking over in a Paddock covered with Buttercups and brushed by a delicious Breeze, while a dainty racing Filly of W. Browne's came startling up to wonder and snuff about me. . . . You would be sorry to think that Omar breathes a sort of Consolation to me! Poor Fellow; I think of him, and Oliver Basselin, and Anacreon; lighter Shadows among the Shades, perhaps, over which Lucretius presides so grimly."

Munro's edition took him back to Lucretius in later years; and he, FitzGerald said, should have been Dante's guide through hell; "but perhaps he was too deep in it, to get out for a Holiday." He adds a note, new so far as I know, of the word *magnus* as the ruling epithet in Lucretius; which is an interesting addition to Shakespeare's "sweet" and Milton's "bright." As to Dante, he tells us a story of a fine answer which Tennyson made to a question of his own, though indeed the question was, in a sense, its own answer.

"We were stopping before a shop in Regent Street, where were two Figures of Dante and

Goethe.   I (I suppose) said, 'What is there in old Dante's Face that is missing in Goethe's?'   And Tennyson (whose Profile then had certainly a remarkable likeness to Dante's) said, 'The Divine.'"

There are some striking stories told of Tennyson, with whom he had such a long friendship, and in whose presence, though he did not always admire his poems, he yet felt "a sense of depression at times from the overshadowing of a so much more lofty intellect than my own."   Here is one:

"Some thirty years ago A. Tennyson went over Burns' Ground in Dumfries.   When he was one day by Doon-side, 'I can't tell how it was, Fitz, but I fell into a Passion of Tears'—and A. T. not given to the melting mood at all."

Tennyson, indeed, evidently impressed him more than any of his contemporaries:

"He *said*, and, I daresay, *says* things to be remembered; decisive Verdicts; which I hope some one makes notes of." . . . "Had I continued to be with him, I would have risked being called another Bozzy by the thankless World, and have often looked in vain for a Note Book I had made of such things."

Everyone will share his regret for the disappearance of that book.   Meanwhile, here is one of the good things which were, happily, not lost with it:

"I daresay I may have told you what Tennyson said of the Sistine Child, which he then knew only by Engraving.   He first thought the Expression of his Face (as also the Attitude) almost too solemn, even for the Christ within.   But some time after, when A. T. was married, and had a Son, he told me that Raffaelle was all right ; that no Man's face was so solemn as a Child's, full of Wonder.   He said one morning that he watched his Babe 'worshipping the Sunbeam on the Bedpost and Curtain.' ”

For most of the poets of his own day he cared little : he detested Browning and Swinburne ; Shelley, as one would expect, he found “ too unsubstantial” for him ; at Wordsworth, “ Daddy Wordsworth,” the “ meeserable poet ” of his Cambridge days, he is always laughing, and then repenting before one of “ those unique things of his, which he brought from the mountains.”   He appreciated Keats much more fully, “ more akin to Shakespeare, I am tempted to think, in a perfect circle of Poetic Faculties, than any Poet since.”   He felt little change in passing from Catullus and Lesbia to Keats and Fanny Brawne (except indeed that terrible name), though he is obliged to add : “ from Catullus' better parts, I mean : for there is too much of filthy and odious—both of Love and Hate.   Oh, my dear Virgil never fell into that : he was fit to be Dante's companion beyond even Purgatory.”

" My dear Virgil "; " my dear Sophocles "; " one loves Virgil somehow " :
that is the way he speaks of the great
ancients. He had the instinct for perfection in these things ; and those who have
that must always look—in these days of
" new " criticism it has become necessary
to repeat it—to that small band, of the very
elect out of every nation, to which Greece
has furnished the largest contribution.
Not that he seems to have returned much
to some of the great Greek poets. For
him Greek poetry meant chiefly Æschylus
and Sophocles : Æschylus, " a dozen lines
of whom have a more Almighty power
on me than all Sophocles' plays "; but
Sophocles as well, because, instead of
" *troubling* us with his grandeur and
gloom," like Æschylus, he is " always
soothing, complete, and satisfactory,"
" the consummation of Greek art."

But *parlons d'autres choses*, as is said so
often in these letters. FitzGerald was not
so occupied with books as to be unable
to find plenty of time for Nature and his
friends. All the old ways of Nature, and
any departure she makes from them, were
observed by him with equal interest :
nothing that goes on in the heavens
escaped his eye ; and when Carlyle saw

Orion at a season during which Orion is in truth not to be seen, he was not fortunate in having FitzGerald for one of his readers. Except for frequent visits to London or Bedfordshire, his life was divided between his home at Boulge or Woodbridge, and places close by them on the Suffolk coast. Neither coast nor inland country is in any way England at her best; but by the seeing eye much may be seen always and anywhere, and the result is that for those who know these letters FitzGerald is, with his own Crabbe, the *genius loci* who is present everywhere. Not that much, or most, of what he says, is not as true of a thousand other places as of Suffolk : it is sheer love of Nature herself, as she is everywhere. He could not bear to be separated from her : hated London for many things, but especially for hiding Nature, and would go to look for her in the Regent's Park or at Hampton Court ; or recall her with his radishes at breakfast, with which " comes a savour of earth that brings all the delicious gardens of the world back into one's soul, and almost draws tears from one's eyes." He had a great enjoyment of art and music, the consolations of life in a great town, but they were not enough for him ; and when he has to be in London, he sits and watches white clouds moving north-east, enjoying the thought that they at any rate are going down to Suffolk. It was not merely London but the Londoners that he hated, detesting nothing so much as the confident and superficial cleverness which is so common in towns. "One finds few in London *serious* men : I mean *serious* even in fun ; with a true purpose and character, whatsoever it may be." He demanded originality too, as well as a fund of seriousness, in the men he was to live with ; and could not find it in London half so well, he thought, as in the country, "where everyone, with whatever natural stock of intellect endowed, at least grows up his own way, and flings his branches about him, not stretched on the *espalier* of London dinner-table company." Frederick Tennyson, who must indeed have been hard to please, complained that his letters had not two ideas in them, and tells him he ought to live in London : to which he sent from Boulge a characteristic *apologia :*

"All I can say is, to say again that, if you lived in this place, you would not write so long a letter as you have done ; though, without any compliment, I am sure you would write a better than

I shall. But you see the original fault in me is that I choose to be in such a place as this at all: that argues certainly a talent for dullness which no situation nor intercourse of men could much improve. It is true: I really do like to sit in this doleful place with a good fire, a cat and a dog on the rug, and an old woman in the kitchen. This is all my live-stock. The house is yet damp, as last year; and the great event of this winter is my putting up a trough round the eaves to carry off the wet. . . . Why should I not live in London and see the world? you say. Why, then, *I* say as before, I don't like it. I think the dullness of country people is better than the impudence of Londoners; and the fresh cold and wet of our clay fields better than a fog that stinks *per se;* and this room of mine, clean at all events, better than a dirty room in Charlotte Street."

He did not "pose" about his way of life, as many men would have done, nor make his philosophic αὐτάρκεια matter of pleasant self-satisfaction.

"Don't suppose I think it good philosophy in myself to keep here out of the world, and sport a gentle Epicurism; I do not; I only follow something of a natural inclination, and know not if I could do better under a more complex system."

Or again, as he writes to Archdeacon Allen:

"I believe I love poetry almost as much as ever; but then I have been suffered to doze all these years in the enjoyment of old childish habits and sympathies, without being called on to more active and serious duties of life. I have not put away childish things, though a man. But, at the same time, this visionary inactivity is better than the mischievous activity of so many I see about me: not better than the useful and virtuous activity of a few others: John Allen among the number."

The fact is, of course, that he knew by instinct the life that suited him, and had the wisdom to refuse to be turned aside from it. If any justification were needed, "Omar" and "Agamemnon" and "Euphranor" and these charming letters, the record of delightful studies, and the picture of a beautiful character, would be more than enough; to say nothing of that humbler vocation, which is all that he ever claimed for himself; as, when writing to Professor Cowell, he says:

"Ten years ago I might have been vext to see you striding along in Sanscrit and Persian so fast: reading so much; remembering all; writing about it so well. But now I am glad to see any man do anything well; and I know that it is my vocation to stand and wait, and know within myself whether it *is* done well."

So he stayed in Suffolk with his books and his music and his country friends;

"no velvet waistcoat and ever-lustrous pumps to be considered: no *bon mots* got up: no information necessary. There is a pipe for the parsons to smoke, and quite as much *bon mots*, literature, and philosophy, as they care for without any trouble at all."

Of course he might have had any society he liked, in London or Suffolk; but he hated seeing new faces in "the polite circles," and much preferred Parson Crabbe coming to spend an evening with him, with a bottle of port under his arm. Of social distinctions he made nothing; he was quite at home among the Woodbridge people, and would go and dine with a carpenter. His early ideal was very much what he attained to: "a small house just outside a pleasant English town, all the days of my life, making myself useful in a humble way, reading my books, and playing a rubber of whist at night." Here is a picture of Woodbridge life which recalls Olney or Weston Underwood: the concluding little laugh at his own literary tastes is just in Cowper's way.

"At Ipswich I pick you up with the washerwoman's pony, and take you to Woodbridge. There Barton sits with the tea already laid out; and Miss about to manage the urn: plain, agreeable people. At Woodbridge, too, is my little friend Churchyard, with whom we shall sup off toasted cheese and porter. Then, last and not least, the sweet retirement of Boulge, where the Graces and Muses, &c."

But, in spite of all this simplicity in social matters, no one ever valued the finer idea of an aristocracy more than FitzGerald. When he says of Plutarch that he must have been a gentleman, he is giving him his highest praise. He was, like Ruskin, " a Tory of the old school, Walter Scott's school, and Homer's," and believed as fervently as Burke in the great qualities of the English gentry. We find him writing from Bedford to Frederick Tennyson :

" The sun shines very bright, and there is a kind of bustle in these clean streets, because there is to be a grand True Blue dinner in the Town-hall. Not that I am going ; in an hour or two I shall be out in the fields, rambling alone. I read Burnet's History—*ex pede Herculem.* Well, say as you will, there is not, and never was, such a country as Old England—never were there such a Gentry as the English. They will be the distinguishing mark and glory of England in History, as the Arts were of Greece, and War of Rome."

But at the same time he thought things were going down the hill, and was severe on the squires of his own day in proportion to his belief in the virtues of their fathers. His indignation is especially stirred up by the cool reception they gave to the Volunteer movement.

"It is a shame the Gentry hereabout are so indifferent in the Matter: they subscribe next to nothing; and give absolutely nothing in the way of Entertainment or Attention to the Corps. But we are split up into the pettiest possible Squirearchy, who want to make the utmost of their little territory: cut down all the Trees, level all the old Violet Banks, and stop up all the Footways they can. The old pleasant way from Hasketon to Bredfield is now a Desert. I was walking it yesterday, and had the pleasure of breaking down and through some Bushes and Hurdles put to block up a fallen Stile. I thought what your Father would have said of it all. And really it is the sad ugliness of our once pleasant Fields that half drives me to the Water, where the Power of the Squirearchy stops."

Perhaps he was happier there than anywhere. On the water, in one way or another—the Ouse in Bedfordshire, his own Deben, and, above all, the sea—he spent a good deal of his time. He could content himself with sailing on the river Deben, "looking at the Crops as they grow green, yellow, russet, and are finally carried away in the red and blue Waggons with the sorrel horse"; or, again, in Browne's house at Bedford, listening to the rustling of the poplars, "which only the Ouse knows how to rear"; till it is time to go and "seek my Piscator, and we shall go to a Village two miles off and fish, and have tea in a pot-house, and so walk home. For all which idle ease I think I must be damned." But, after all, peace and contentment may come of rivers : delight and passion belong to the sea, who brooks no rivals near her throne. Certainly she had none in FitzGerald's heart, and for him the " one merit of the little dull country town on whose border I live is an Estuary that brings up Tidings of the Sea "; the thing to be remembered in a return journey from Scotland is the glimpse of sea at Berwick; Lowestoft is " very ugly," and its " herring-pond " will not do after the Atlantic, but "still it is— The Sea"; Suffolk is "redeemed from dulness" by being near the sea, and allowing its inhabitants to catch a glimpse of it from the tops of hills and of houses ; and even at Boulge, ten miles away, he must open his window at night, when the wind lay that way, and manage somehow to hear it, whether in fact or in fancy. The sea, he finds, "somehow talks to one of old things "; so that he will write more often to Mrs. Kemble from Lowestoft than from elsewhere, will try to get an old sweetheart of his to come and walk with him on the beach at Aldeburgh, and take his best book friends with him on his little yacht, Crabbe and Don Quixote, Dante "who atones with the sea," and above all the great Greeks. For "it is wonderful," he says, how the sea brings up an "appetite for Greek: it likes to be called θάλασσα and πόντος better than the wretched word '*Sea*,' I am sure: and the Greeks (especially Æschylus—after Homer) are full of Seafaring Sounds and Allusions. I think the Murmur of the Ægean (if that is their Sea) wrought itself into their Language."

But I must make an end of quotations, and leave a hundred bits of humour or poetry, unseen or seen only in a momentary glance: his yacht the *Scandal*, so called because it was "the staple product of Woodbridge"; the church at Boulge, where "fungi grow in great numbers about the communion table," and where "Parson and Clerk get through the service see-saw, like two men in a saw-pit"; his boy-reader who "ate such a Quantity of Cheese and Cake between the Acts that he could scarce even see to read at all after," and had to be reminded "that though he was not quite sixteen, he had much exceeded the years of a Pig; since which we get on better"; the rustics of Boulge and Debach, whom he taught to sing; the trees, "which all magnanimous Men respect and love," and the squires who cut them down and move Parson Crabbe to cry out, "How *scanda*lously they misuse the Globe!"; the winter picture of the "poor mistaken lilac-buds, there out of the window, and an old Robin, ruffled up to his thickest, sitting mournfully under them, quite disheartened"; and the spring picture which makes him "abjure all Authorship, contented with the divine Poem which Great Nature is now composing about us," till he comes to think "no man ever grew so old as not to feel younger in Spring." All these and much else I must leave, or hurry by, only hoping that I have quoted enough to make all who care for good sense and good English, heightened often by a dash of poetry, go and search these charming letters for themselves.

Delightful perhaps as FitzGerald's letters are, he will hardly take equal rank with our very finest English letter-writers. To be a classic of the first order in any kind of writing, style is needed,—style not only of occasional or frequent perfection, such as is to be found in these letters, but assured, sustained, unfailing, such as Gray and Cowper, without ceasing for one moment to be natural and simple, had always at command. Ease and naturalness are indeed the first of qualities in a writer of letters; but they can be pushed too far, at least in letters that come to be published. FitzGerald was in the habit of doing what he liked, and saying what he liked with his friends, and sometimes, it seems, carried his liberty to considerable lengths, so that we smile at finding Mrs. Kemble obliged to complain of his putting his tumbler on the floor in her house. It is the same in his letters. There is nothing indeed for his friends to complain of; but for the public, reading them collected in a book, it cannot but be that they will now and then be felt to pass the bounds which separate the easy from the free and easy. There is just too much of the odd, and the interjectional, and the spasmodic about them to let them strike our ears with quite the same note of perfection which sounds in Cowper's Letters, or Gray's.

But when that has been said, all, perhaps too much, is said. No one could write better English than FitzGerald, when he chose, as "Euphranor" proves; and there are a thousand things in these

letters to prove it too. It is only as a
whole that he need yield to any one, and
then only to the very best. And, after all,
the chief interest of letters lies, as I have
said, in the personality they reveal ; and to
many tastes that of FitzGerald, racier and
richer than Cowper, easier than Gray,
larger, if there were nothing else, than
Lamb, will prove a rare, or even a unique
attraction. No one, at any rate, can
altogether miss his charm : so cheerful as
he is and so kindly, so absolutely healthy
and human and genuine, a man made up
of good blood and bone within, and fresh
English air from land and sea without,
whose friendships were " like loves," and
extended not only to men and women, but
to beasts and birds and flowers.

In this last point, as in a some others,
he has now and then reminded me of
a French poet whom, curiously enough,
he did not like, La Fontaine. Fitz-
Gerald's taste in literature was for the
large and easy style of Scott and
Cervantes; and La Fontaine's gift of
delicate and detailed perfection was, in
the main, lost upon him. But it is
strange that he felt no touch of affinity
for the man, whose friendships had the
rare depth and Roman constancy of his

own; who chose, like himself, from the first to stand apart from the crowd, and watch and dream and judge instead of acting; whose interviews with lawyers were as tiresome and fruitless as his; whose poetic sympathies saw, as he did, life and feeling everywhere, and who could be happiest, as he was, in a world peopled only by trees and birds. No one indeed could quite say of La Fontaine, what was said of FitzGerald when he died, "a very noble character has passed away." But FitzGerald was no harsh judge of human sins or frailties; and in the Elysian fields at least let us hope that they have become acquainted, and enjoy together there the delight of dreaming out long summer days, which each loved so well when he breathed earthly air above.

THE END.

BRADBURY, AGNEW, & CO. LD., PRINTERS, LONDON AND TONBRIDGE.

www.ingramcontent.com/pod-product-compliance
Lightning Source LLC
Chambersburg PA
CBHW031033120726
47905CB00007B/2161